The Lord is my strength
and my shield, in whom
my heart trusted and found help.
So my heart rejoices; with my
song I praise my God.
Psalm 28:7

The intent and
purpose of this volume is to
give you faith, hope and
inspiration. Hopefully it will help bring
peace and tranquility into your life. May
it be a reminder of God's love, guidance
and His many blessings.

Our publications help to support our work
for needy children in over 120 countries
around the world. Through our
programs, thousands of children are
fed, clothed, educated, sheltered
and given the opportunity to
live decent lives.

Salesian Missions wishes to extend special thanks and gratitude to our generous poet friends and to the publishers who have given us permission to reprint material included in this book. Every effort has been made to give proper acknowledgments. Any omissions or errors are deeply regretted, and the publisher, upon notification, will be pleased to make the necessary corrections in subsequent editions.

Cover photo: © Medio Images/Fotosearch Stock Photography

First Edition Printed in the U.S.A. by Concord Litho Group, Concord, NH 03301.

A Song Within My Heart
from the
Salesian Collection

Compiled and Edited
by Jennifer Grimaldi

Illustrated by
Bob Pantelone, Frank Massa, Gail L. Pepin,
Russell Bushée, Terrie Meider, Helen M. L. Kunic,
Maureen McCarthy, Paul Scully, Dale Begley
and Robert VanSteinburg

Contents

The Blessedness of Quiet Times

The blessedness of quiet times
When God and I commune
With morning sunshine touching soft
Or gentle breeze at noon.
In whispered prayer, the evening stars
Speak of His loving power,
And in the silence of the night,
He's with me every hour.
The blessedness of quiet times
Comes in the dance of Spring,
When Summer flowers start to bloom,
When Autumn colors bring…

The cold north wind of Winter's chill
When snowdrifts start to form;
The love God burns into my heart –
His fire keeps me warm.
The blessedness of quiet times,
When God and I can share.
The love He gives, in many ways,
Is with me everywhere.

Nancy Watson Dodrill

Just Keep Your Eyes on Jesus

It's easy to be tempted,
To take the path that's wrong.
Just keep your eyes on Jesus
And He will make you strong.

So often friends may fail you
And turn and walk away.
Just keep your eyes on Jesus –
He's there both night and day.

And when you're at a total loss,
When everything seems bleak,
Just keep your eyes on Jesus
And listen to Him speak.

Helen Parker

The Many Wonders

Walk with me as I wander
Through the forest, glen, or glade,
Seeking out the many wonders
That our Lord above has made...

Tiny lilies of the valley,
Majestic trees and mountains steep,
All the glories of the heavens
And the earth beneath our feet.

And the beauty that we're seeing
Makes our hearts beat wild with joy,
Just knowing God made these wonders
For His children to enjoy.

But more than that He gives us comfort
As we travel on life's way,
Guides our footsteps lest we falter,
Leads us safely through each day.

Gertrude Blau Byram

*Know that the Lord works
wonders for the faithful; the
Lord hears when I call out.*
Psalm 4:4

9

Pretty Pictures

God paints such pretty pictures
From the dawn 'til set of sun;
Our pleasures could be endless
If we'd count them one by one.

Take time to greet the morning
And see the Master's touch,
Surrounding us with splendor
In things we love so much.

The sky of blue, the rose so fair,
The sun that gives us light,
The robin's song, the misty dew –
Each manifests His might.

The sounds, sights, and scents of life
Are blessings from above,
To every child who takes the time
To recognize His love.

Give thanks to our Creator
For the beauty of each day;
Our world He fills with wonder
As we journey on our way.

A lifetime filled with beauty,
Captive memories we have won.
For our delights and pleasures,
He should hear us say, "Well done!"

Shirley Takacs

Without the Rain

Without the rain, we wouldn't know
The scent of Summer flowers.
Without the pain, how could we feel
The depth of joyful hours?
Without the light, how could we see
The beauty that surrounds us?
Without the dark, how could the light's
Bright glory shine around us?
Without a friend, how could we be
A friend, in truth, to others?
Without God's love within our hearts,
We'd never love our brothers.
Whate'er life brings – good or bad,
May it be joy or sorrows –
His grace and neverending love
Will bless all our tomorrows.

Vi B. Chevalier

In His Loving Hands

We know not what tomorrow brings,
Although we plan ahead,
For only God alone can know
The pathway we must tread.

We cannot know the future,
Not one minute nor one hour.
Each circumstance that we must face
Lay only in His power.

It's vital that we live by faith
From minute unto minute
And trust that every step we take
He's walking with us in it.

This alone should give us hope –
Whatever be our plans –
In knowing that our future lies
In His sweet, loving hands.

Betty Purser Patten

Into Your hands I commend
my spirit; You will redeem
me, Lord, faithful God.
Psalm 31:6

So Good

My God is so good to me!
I thank Him every day
For blessings that He gives to me
All along life's way.

He gives many precious friends
Who understand and care,
And every time I need His help
I know He hears my prayer.

He knows how often I would fall
Were He not by my side.
So He sends His Holy Spirit
To be my constant guide.

His love is greater than I know!
He's happy to forgive,
And then He wants to help me
In obedience to live.

My God is very good to me!
I hope you know Him, too.
For all the things He does for me
He wants to do for you.

Vera Beall Parker

15

The Little Voice Inside

I'm tempted to put off the task,
Relax and let it slide.
"Just do it. You'll feel better,"
Prompts the little voice inside.

I know I should apologize,
Forget my foolish pride;
I hear a gentle coaxing
From the little voice inside.

The struggle seems all uphill
Even though I've tried and tried.
"Don't quit. You're going to make it,"
Says the little voice inside.

So always stop and listen.
Let your conscience be your guide.
The Holy Spirit's speaking
Through the little voice inside.

Karen Taylor

*We have not received the spirit of the
world but the Spirit that is from
God, so that we may understand
the things freely given us by God.*
1 Corinthians 2:12

Arise, north wind! Come, south wind!
Blow upon my garden that its
perfumes may spread abroad...
Song 4:16

The Master Gardener

God's working within us,
This we know is true,
In ways not so obvious
To me and to you.
We're constantly changing
Though our eyes can't see
All the newness within us –
In you and in me.
But slowly God works
In the garden of our hearts,
Pulling the weeds
So the flowers may start.
He tends to the garden
With such love and deep care
And delights with each blossom
He finds blooming there.
He never stops tending
The garden inside
'Til blooms fill the spaces
Where weeds did once hide.
And though we can't see it,
We're changing – it's true!
The gardener is working
Within me, within you.
He's tending and mending
And bringing new life
Whether your garden is joyous
Or filled up with strife.
If we'll keep our hands out,
He'll keep His hands in
And He'll bring forth beauty
From your garden within.

Gina Mazzullo Laurin

Safe Harbor

Our life on earth is oh, so short –
Just a blink in endless time,
But the life we'll live with Jesus
Is everlasting and divine.

Compare it to the ocean waves –
Some are high, while others low,
But with Jesus as our pilot,
He will lift and help us grow.

Our vessel will be overflowing
With His blessings from above,
'Til at last we reach safe harbor,
Surrounded in His arms of love.

Albert N. Theel

Solitude

Solitude is something precious
That one cherishes at times,
Just an hour or a moment –
Needed seconds to unwind.

Blessed solace and contentment,
Peaceful moments of the day,
Precious is the time, Master,
You allow for me to pray.

Tranquil at the twilight's calling
When I close my eyes in sleep,
Just to know that I am safely
In the Master's loving keep.

Katherine Smith Matheney

*My soul shall savor the rich
banquet of praise, with joyous lips
my mouth shall honor You!*
Psalm 63:6

The Master of My Fate

He is the Master of my fate –
He knows what's best for me.
I stand at His command and wait
To learn my destiny.

Two roads He gave me in my life,
Two ways in which to go.
One led to darkness and to strife
And one to sunshine's glow.

I took the wrong road at the start,
Not giving it much thought,
But soon I learned with heavy heart
The pain that it had brought.

But then, I saw just up ahead
A sign in letters bold;
A crossroad that I took instead
And there, found joy untold.

'Twas there I met my Savior;
He helped me understand
That life is sweet where'er we meet
If you but hold His hand.

He is the Master of my fate –
He knows what's best for me.
No longer do I stand and wait...
I found my destiny!

Lou Ella Cullipher

The View From His Window

Tender boughs gently swaying
In cool breezes, lightly playing,
Under skies of cobalt blue,
Below the sun, a molten hue,
Beneath the heavens' gracious light…
Purest beauty in God's sight.

Rebecca Sweeney

A Friend Indeed

Each day I venture on my way
To face the problems of the day,
And find that I am not alone,
As God's love and grace have shown.

All that I need do is ask
For His help with each hard task
To find I have a Friend indeed,
As He helps me to succeed.

He steers me at a steady pace
Through life's sometimes hectic race,
Helping me to not be blind
To the needs of all mankind.

Though sometimes I'm unaware
That His presence lingers there,
I'm certain by the close of day
That His love had come my way.

Catherine Janssen Irwin

A Prayer of Hope

Dear God, our help in ages past,
Our hope from day to day,
Look down upon this troubled world
And lead us, Lord, we pray.

We're traveling through some stormy nights,
Our hearts are heavy still.
We pray that You will heal our land
According to Your will.

Please help us to confess our sins
And turn to You today.
With You, dear God, to lead us
We'll surely find our way.

Shirley W. Langley

*Be strong and take heart, all
you who hope in the Lord.*
Psalm 31:25

He Knows Me

Oh Lord, I am an open book –
You know my every thought.
You know when I'm contented
Or when I am distraught.

Your presence forever surrounds me;
There is nothing You don't see.
You're always there to guide me,
Even though my will is free.

You know the numbers of my hair
And what lies within my heart.
You know what words I plan to speak
Well before I even start.

Oh Lord, I just can't comprehend
The love You have for me.
I see Your hand in everything
That has been or will ever be.

Shirley Hile Powell

*I will praise You, Lord, with
all my heart; I will declare all
Your wondrous deeds.*
Psalm 9:2

The Morning

The morning is a splendid time
To tell God of your love;
A splendid time to praise Him for
All blessings from above.

Just thank Him for your night of sleep
And precious hours of rest,
And thank Him for the cozy home
With which your family's blessed.

And thank Him for the time of prayer
That opens up your day,
And for the sunshine or the rain,
Whatever comes your way.

And thank Him for the food He sends
In this blest land of ours,
And thank Him for the songs of birds
And fragrant, lovely flowers.

Do thank Him for your health and strength
To finish every task,
And for the answers to your prayers
When in Christ's name you ask.

And thank Him for salvation, too,
For Jesus so divine,
Who gave His life on Calvary
To cleanse your sins and mine.

In adoration and in love
Lift up your words of praise,
Then you will find His gift of peace
And joy throughout your days.

Katherine Tappa

These Things, O Lord, I Ask of Thee

This my daily prayer will be;
These things, O Lord, I ask of Thee –
Strength to face the trials I'll meet,
Faith to accomplish the goals I seek,
Hope to keep my vision bright,
Courage in the darkest night.
Smiles to brighten a gloomy day,
Laughter to chase the blues away,
Trust to keep my thinking sound,
Abounding love to pass around.

Ruth Moyer Gilmour

Blessings

I've health and home and family;
That's plain for all to see.
I count each as a blessing,
For God's so good to me!

When cooking in the kitchen
Or drifting on the sea,
I have that peaceful feeling,
For God's so good to me!

Secure within His wisdom,
I'll follow faithfully,
By love and peace surrounded,
For God's so good to me!

Now looking to the future,
Contented I will be,
So long as He is leading,
For God's so good to me!

Anna M. Matthews

*Then the Lord looked
upon the earth, and filled
it with His blessings.*
Sirach 16:27

Keep Me Strong

Lord, help me to accept
The changes that you bring,
And if my heart should break,
Help me endure the sting.

Let me learn and grow from
Each and every test;
Help me keep my faith and
Leave to You the rest.

Help me to sing praises
Whatever comes my way,
Knowing "this shall pass," and
There'll be a brighter day.

Help me to hold on to
What You have done before,
When You pierced the darkness
And opened up the door.

Letting in the sunshine
Of Your blessed love,
Filling me with peace that
Comes only from above.

You've not failed me yet, Lord;
I know You never will,
And when my faith is weak,
I know You love me still.

So hold my hand – keep me strong
Whatever comes my way.
When my tears begin to fall,
Let me stop to pray.

And may Your precious name
Be glorified through me.
May I reflect Your love so
Others are drawn to Thee.

Denise A. DeWald

Faith, Hope, and Love

Faith is my treasure
That glitters like gold.
It fills up my heart
And runs through my soul.
Though worries surround me,
Oh God, I will wait.
Despair and confusion
Will soon pass away.

Hope springs eternal
Behind all my cares.
Though I feel sadness,
I know God's aware.
I wait for His guidance
And look for His signs,
Above and below,
In front and behind.

Love is my teacher
Beyond what I see.
God in His mercy
Won't forget me.
Though troubles abound
And fill me with fear,
Soon comes tomorrow,
And then God appears.

John Frederick Zurn

*So faith, hope, love
remain, these three; but the
greatest of these is love.*
1 Corinthians 13:13

While There Is Time

When we come to the end of that long, long road,
No matter how clever or shrewd
We've been through the years, how will we react
When the book of our lives is viewed?
Whatever success we have managed to gain,
In spite of each brilliant degree,
What do you suppose His judgement will be
When God looks inside you and me?

For it isn't the money we have in the bank,
The prudent investments we prize,
It isn't our status among the elite
That counts for a thing in His eyes.
When we entered this world we had not a shred,
And we'll not take a thing when we leave,
Depending upon the seeds we have sown,
The welcome we're apt to receive.

So while there is time let us see to the things
We cannot afford to neglect,
And by all the good we can possibly do,
Insure the reward we expect.
For moments are fleeting; it may be today,
MIght be the last one you shall see –
And we must have an answer, for Jesus will ask,
"What have you accomplished for Me?"

Grace E. Easley

The Ringing
Of the Church Bells

The ringing of the church bells
Upon the Sabbath day,
Beckons me to worship
And offer thanks and pray.
As I sit within these sacred walls,
I feel that God is near
To strengthen and sustain me
And fill my heart with cheer.
As I leave the house of worship,
I feel within my heart
My life is far more brighter
Because God is a part.

Harold F. Mohn

Little Prayers

As we pass a fellow man
Who is burdened low,
We can say a little prayer
For God to bless him so.
And if we hear of someone's need,
Though distant from our place,
A little prayer upon our lips
Will not decrease our pace.
For little prayers are helpful
When tasks won't let us pause,
But we can wish and pray in heart
For others' needs and cause.
The prayers may just be simple
As we seek life's best
For those who ache and suffer,
We wish to see them blest.
So let us fill some moments
Of every busy day
With lots of special little prayers
And send them on their way.

Virginia Borman Grimmer

Answer when I call, my saving God.
In my troubles, You cleared a way;
show me favor; hear my prayer.
Psalm 4:2

Memories

Our Creator's in our corner
Each moment of each day,
Standing by to guide us
In His own special way.

We must always be thankful
For our dear Savior up above.
He showers us with riches
And His unconditional love.

Through Him we have our parents
Who are always standing by
To be our constant example.
It's with them our blessings lie.

Time has a way of reliving.
Growing older, we reminisce
With thoughts of our dear families
And the softness of each kiss.

Our fortune is our families
Made possible through our King.
No money on earth can ever buy
The love their smiles bring.

Yes, these lovely things He's provided
To make our lifetime sweet,
And none can ever be replaced…
These moments make life complete.

Dixie L. Little

The favors of the Lord I will recall,
the glorious deeds of the Lord, because of
all He has done for us…
Isaiah 63:7

Snowfall

Wisps of snow sailing 'round,
Softly fall to the frozen ground;
They look like diamonds lying there,
Sparkling ice-jewels of beauty rare.
Beautiful gifts that fall from the sky
Are snowflaked gifts you cannot buy.
Windows ice-coated with frost-fringed lace
Have filigree frosting all over their face.
Snow-capped mountains stand serene
To set this glorious Winter scene.
When ice and snow are in their prime
Beautiful is God's wintertime.

Nora M. Bozeman

Thank You, Lord

Thank You, Lord, for loving us
No matter what our ways.
Thank You, Lord, for staying near
Until our end of days.
Thank You, Lord, for answering us
Each moment that we call.
Thank You, Lord, for giving us
Gifts both great and small.
Thank You, Lord, for keeping us
Safe from every harm,
And thank You, Lord, for holding us
So gently in Your arms.

Eva Marie Ippolito

*We thank You, God, we give
thanks; we call upon Your name,
declare Your wonderful deeds.*
Psalm 75:2

Prayer of Hope

God, please help me find my way
And give me room to grow.
Comfort me through every storm
And guide me as I go.

My heart is weary time to time
From living all alone.
I need You to be with me –
Please make Your presence known.

Life can sometimes take a turn
Upon a rocky road.
I get worried and afraid
To face this heavy load.

Help me find an even ground
To carry out Your will.
Let me find a purpose, Lord,
Your promise to fulfill.

And may I never fall apart
Nor take my eyes off You.
I am weak, but You are strong –
Please show me what to do.

I give You thanks for this good day,
No matter how I fare.
For You, dear Lord, have heard my plea;
My pain is Yours to bear.

Jill Lemming LeBlanc

*May your kindness, Lord,
be upon us; we have put
our hope in You.*
Psalm 33:22

Because He Loves Us

In the early morning stillness,
In the early morning light,
When swallows are beginning
Their early morning flight,
Before the golden sunshine
Caresses land and sea,
God's everlasting presence
Blesses you and me,
For He is with us always
To help us chart each day,
And if we turn to Him with faith,
He'll lead us all the way.

Vi B. Chevalier

*He set me free in
the open; He rescued me
because He loves me.*
Psalm 18:20

47

Happiness

Don't fret about tomorrow,
For today has just begun.
Each morning is a new day –
Make each day a special one.

When you give a simple smile
Or a neighborly hello,
Sometimes that is all it takes
To make your morning glow.

The happiness you spread
Or the confidence you show
Returns two-fold in others
And the whole world seems to know.

Your misfortunes seem to lessen
When you smile instead of cry.
All the happiness you covet
Seems to spread to passers-by.

Set your goals toward the positive,
In yourself and in others, too.
Then all your hardships will be easier
And more happiness will shine through.

Gloria Swan Kennedy

Little Church Across the Meadow

The little church across the meadow
Greets me each and every morn,
As I glance out through my window
On a day that's just been born.

Shining in the morning sun
So steadfast, strong, and true,
Tall steeple reaching to the sky,
My spirit lifts anew.

Each time I see it standing there,
I know within my heart
That God's love is always with us
And will never, ever part.

Lola Neff Merritt

A Time to Pray

The dawn breaks forth,
Shedding light on earth;
A new beginning
Has given birth.
A time to rejoice
As we meet the day;
Down on our knees –
'Tis a time to pray.
'Tis the hour of noon;
A time to pause,
To refresh, meditate
On His holy laws,
Asking strength to serve
The rest of the day,
To praise and thank
'Tis a time to pray.
'Tis the hour of dusk,
That tranquil hour
When rest comes to all –
Man, creature, and flower.
A time to give thanks
For guiding our way,
To express our love –
'Tis a time to pray.
'Tis evening now,
And in weariness
We look to Him
For blessed rest,
Sending our every
Care His way,
Down on our knees –
'Tis a time to pray.

Helen Gleason

Just When

Just when the burdens of life were most heavy,
Just when it seemed I was close to despair,
God gently lifted each one of my burdens,
Making them lighter, more easy to bear.

Just when it seemed that my life was most happy,
Sorrow came knocking again at my door.
Heartsick and weary, my hopes seemed to shatter –
Gone were the dreams I had worked so hard for.

Just when it seemed that the sun had ceased shining,
Just when I felt that's just how it would be,
There in the sky shone God's beautiful rainbow
Sending His promise of hope back to me.

Just when I needed that hope and assurance,
Just when such loneliness engulfed my days,
God touched my heart and with loving compassion
Whispered, "My child, I am with you always."

Knowing this truth, I can face each tomorrow.
God will not give me more than I can bear.
He knows the "just whens" and He will deliver –
Great is His faithfulness, mercy and care.

Beverly J. Anderson

Beauty

Physical beauty is fleeting –
An illusion of youth and of years.
'Tis the beauty of soul that never grows old;
It increases through life's joy and tears.

Youth's beauty blooms just for a moment
And fades with the setting of sun,
But the beauty of soul is a treasure untold,
Growing richer as life's race is run.

Nona Mae Coone

It's Not Too Late
For Today

It's not too late for today;
Don't put it off 'til tomorrow.
If you have made some mistakes,
Confess them now and grace will follow.

Don't gamble with life eternal.
You must repent; this you know.
Take a vow to make amends,
And a new beginning shall follow.

Humbly admit you did wrong.
Joy will return and you'll find
All of your sins are forgiven.
Then you will have peace of mind.

And forget all worldly gain;
Just embrace your sacred vow.
It's not too late for today,
So talk to the Lord right now!

Edna Massimilla

See God's Wonders With Your Heart

Every morning in the wee daylight hours,
I find peace that lingers through the day.
And humbly, I replenish my spirit
While reverently to God I pray.

For the moment, I forget all my troubles,
Concentrate on what is to come;
I envision a palace of glory
Where I'll rest when life's battle is won.

While I listen to melodies of songbirds,
Merrily flitting through each shiny, green tree,
I can almost hear God's voice among them,
Making known His great blessings for me.

Sitting there with my eyes closed in reverence
Of One who loved me from the start,
I realize that sight is not needed,
For I'm seeing God's wonders with my heart!

Mary S. Chevalier

You alone are the God who did
wonders; among the peoples You
revealed Your might.
Psalm 77:15

Flicker of Memories

In memory, I walk through woods
And I see blooming there
Wildflowers in their varied hues
While fragrance fills the air.

I hear the soothing rhythm of
Small streams that make their way
O'er rocks they've splashed for centuries
And never once did stray.

I hear the symphony of birds –
Each species sings its song,
All blend into a melody –
For times gone past, I long.

I feel warm rays of sunshine as
They filter down through leaves,
And as I reach a clearing, I
Can feel a cooling breeze.

And as it washes o'er my face
And I tread days of yore,
A sudden warmth tugs at my heart –
I've felt that force before.

And then at night when stars appear
Like diamonds set in blue,
My mind drifts back to times long past –
More scenes come into view.

'Twas then old memories did fade,
For as I counted sheep,
A moonbeam gently stroked my face
And I was fast asleep.

Luther Elvis Albright

Life's Journey

There can be a brighter side
To every rainy day
If you place your trust in Jesus
As you travel 'long life's way.

So perk up your ambitions,
Aiming for the sky,
And focus on that rainbow –
Don't lifelong dreams deny.

Take time along the highways
To see the beauty there,
Finding little pleasures,
Never bowing to despair.

Don't overlook the back roads,
For it's there you'll find
Friendship, love, and kinship –
Those sweet rewards of time.

Catherine Janssen Irwin

Together

Whenever it feels like you're all alone
And no one seems to care,
And even the sun refuses to shine,
God is always there.

When trouble comes knocking and no one can help,
And there seems to be no easy way out,
God is beside you to hear all your prayers,
And to cast out your confusion and doubt.

For all of the troubles are reasons to need Him,
They come to you right from His hand;
Meant to be too much to bear all alone,
Just the way that He planned.

When you pray and things come together,
There is no question at all.
You never were suffering all by yourself...
God waited and hoped you would call.

Margaret Peterson

Seaside Longings

Walking along the sandy shore,
My heart is touched by all I see –
The swishing of the ocean's waves,
Lapping aimlessly and free;
The honking of the seagulls
And the rushing of the shore
Floods my soul with seaside longings –
Oh, tell me what more could be in store?
Shiny stones and off-shaped seashells,
Awesome treasures left behind,
Polished to perfection –
Souvenirs to excite one's mind.

A lighthouse in the distance
With a bright beam to light the way
Calls out to me to wonder
And set my sails today.
A sunset resting overhead
With soft colors to behold
Sets my heart once more to dreaming
Though the night be damp and cold.
God understands our seaside longings,
So He created this very special place
Of leaping ocean waters,
Tranquility and grace.

Linda C. Grazulis

I wait with longing for the Lord,
my soul waits for His word.
Psalm 130:5

Treasures

These, my treasures, here are told –
Precious things, most dear, I hold.
Heart beat quickens! Memories...
Turn once more the golden key,
Calling forth the stored delight,
Pansies smiling in sun's light;
Children's play, a creek, a hill,
Evening song of whippoorwill
Closing out a summer day;
Family gathered close, to pray.
Grace abounding to impart
God's sweet treasures to my heart.

Anna Lee Edwards McAlpin

Peace

Peace in my heart – this is my prayer;
Quiet contentment to have and to share
Each new tomorrow, blessed and real,
Each wondrous dawning, a daybreak ideal.

Peace in my home, this I would ask;
Sharing each burden to lighten our task.
Laughter abundant, so much that's worthwhile;
Faith, hope and courage – a bright, happy smile.

Peace in this country, this is my dream;
Peace we might cherish – joyous, supreme,
No more of hatred, no more of crime;
Peacefulness only, in your heart and mine.

Peace in our world, this is my prayer;
With one God to guide us and one God to care.
All of us neighbors, then surely we'll see
That peace is the answer to eternity.

Garnett Ann Schultz

May He grant you
joy of heart and may peace
abide among you...
Sirach 50:23

65

The Gift of Sight

I made a list of precious gifts
That God has granted me;
Among them is the gift of sight,
That beauty I might see.

The rolling hills, the meadowland,
Lemoned with dandelion;
The greening trees, the blooming shrubs,
The sun that sends its shine.

The springtime showers with droplets small,
A rainbow on its heels;
Flowers peeping through the sod,
The season's seeded fields.

The songbirds with their lilting tunes
When Summer fills the land;
The crimson sunsets in the west,
Designed by God's own hand.

The Autumn splashed with vibrant hues
Of russet, orange, red, gold;
The Winter with its flakes of snow
As a wonderland unfolds.

I made a list of cherished gifts
Which God has given me.
Lord, thank You for the gift of life
And, too, for eyes to see.

Loise Pinkerton Fritz

A Name Above All Others

There's a name above all others
That is music to my ears;
One that makes my heart sing happily
All throughout my earthly years.
It's the precious name of Jesus
That my soul longs to hear.
There is no other name more precious;
There is no other name so dear.
When I speak the name of Jesus,
I bow my head in prayer
And thank Him for His blessings
And for His loving care.

Shirley Hile Powell

New Tomorrow

We build a new tomorrow
By the deeds we do today
That are of good or bad
And the words we choose to say.
So, what we do and say today –
In honesty or jest –
Will be our cross or crown of joy
When dawn of day is blessed.

Each deed of kindness or of sin
That we commit today
Will build our new tomorrow
As a sad or happy day.
And we cannot improve our deeds
With Heaven's dawning rays –
We will be heirs to what we did
And what we said today.

Michael Dubina

Bless the Lord, O my soul,
and forget not all His benefits.
Psalm 103:2

An Apple-blossom Morning

Today I come with no requests;
My thankful heart must be expressed.
An apple-blossom morning sent
Now fills me with a sweet content.

In leafy treetop somewhere near,
A robin sings his morning cheer.
Pretty flowers, wee faces bright,
Can't help but bring your heart delight.

A fresh new scent on dew-drenched air
Gives hint of lilacs wondrous fair,
Brought indoors their rich perfume
Makes heavenly the plainest room.

Fluffy white clouds on sky of blue
Bids we take the upward view,
And I in awesome wonder see
God's splendor and His majesty.

With all this beauty and much more,
So many things I'm thankful for:
My home and family, each friend dear,
Blessings heaped high throughout the year.

Lord, forgive me when I seek Your door
Asking for just one thing more.

Kay Hoffman

In Moments of Prayer

May we walk the path of life
In our Redeemer's care,
Daily glorifying Him with praise
In our moments of prayer,
Asking Him for guidance
As we journey through our days,
To have Him walk beside us
And beckon when we stray.
May He then help us to follow
His path of light once more
Until we reach His gateway,
His kingdom and His door.

Jacqui Richardson

Life's Worth

As I look back upon the years,
The time I've spent on earth,
I recall both joy and tears
And evaluate life's worth.

Did I serve God along the way
And help my fellow man
Or did I think only of myself
And fail to understand?

If I pass through this way but once,
Accepting all life's gifts,
Then I must also do my share
To show my thanks for His.

Dolores Karides

*For I long to see you, that I may share
with you some spiritual gift so that
you may be strengthened.*
Romans 1:11

Family Ties

Spend some time with your children –
Set time aside each day
To talk with them and listen
To what they have to say.
Spend some time reading stories
Or hiking here and there,
And before they go to bed,
Spend some time in prayer.

Go on picnics in the Summer
And fly a kite or two,
Sow seeds to start a garden
And see what God can do!
Take in a local ball game
And root for the home team,
And go fishing now and then
In a nearby pond or stream.
Spend some time with your children –
It's always time well spent,
For one day before you know it,
You'll wonder where they went!

Clay Harrison

Let Go

Let go of the anger,
Let go of the pain;
Sunshine will follow
After the rain.

Let go of your worry,
Let go of your fears;
You can't see the rainbow
With your eyes full of tears.

Just let it all go
Like leaves in the wind,
Then follow the Savior
And you'll find peace, my friend.

Steven Michael Schumacher

*...The Lord God will wipe away the
tears from all faces; The reproach of His
people He will remove from the whole
earth; for the Lord has spoken.*
Isaiah 25:8

Blue Shadows

Blue shadows gently fall across
Dusk's snow-white, sculptured fields,
As a Winter sun casts feeble rays
Before the daylight yields.

Leafless trees march straight and tall
In blankets virgin white;
Silent sentinels standing guard
Through Winter's cold, still night.

Lola Neff Merritt

The Lord is my light and
my salvation – whom shall I fear?
Psalm 27:1

Whom Shall I Fear?

Whom shall I fear when temptation comes
And knocks upon my door?
My faith in God is stronger now
Than it's ever been before.

The powers of darkness can't prevail
Where God has shed His light,
For He shall be my rock and shield
Against the coming night.

The shepherd knows His frightened sheep
May sometimes go astray,
But He won't rest until they're found
And brought back to the way.

Through shadowed vales and mountains high,
I know I'm not alone;
I've built my house on solid rock
With faith the cornerstone.

Where, oh, the end is now thy sting?
Vanquished evermore!
Whom shall I fear when temptation comes
And knocks upon my door?

Clay Harrison

Jesus Is Alive

I see the world around me
As a place where I can grow,
Caring and sharing on my way,
Wherever I may go.

With God as my Restorer,
Redeemer and my Friend,
The road ahead is smoother
With the love He freely sends.

Whatever lies before me,
I know I will survive.
My hope is in the promise
That Jesus is alive.

Jill Lemming LeBlanc

When Comfort Is Needed

May God's Spirit flow through me
As I journey down life's road
To help those in trouble
By lightening their load.

When comfort is needed,
May I always be there
To provide strength and love
To those in bitter despair.

When life's trials are many
And some lose their way,
Let me help God to find them
And guide them each day.

At the end of the evening
When I fall to my knees,
Let me pray and thank God
For giving others some ease.

Shirley Hile Powell

Quiet Times

Everybody needs a break
From the pressures of the day;
We need to take some quiet time
To meditate and pray.

Reflecting on our blessings
Will restore vitality,
Communicating with our Lord
Releases all anxiety.

Sit back – relax – and close your eyes,
Then let God's blessings flow.
Feel His loving arms enfold you
As you bask within His glow.

Open up your heart and mind
In the quiet time you spend,
Relinquishing your anguish
And the problems that offend.

God restores you with His love –
He renews your energy,
His everlasting promises
Promote tranquility.

Acknowledge Him and praise His name;
Trust that He will guide you.
Reach out with utmost reverence,
For God Is there beside you.

Patience Allison Hartbauer

*My people will live in peaceful
country, in secure dwellings
and quiet resting places.*
Isaiah 32:18

Family Gatherings

There's nothing more precious
Than family and friends,
The love of tradition
I hope never ends.
Memories of yesterday
Will surely live on
Long after a number
Of us will be gone.
So, cherish the moment…
Make memories each day
And thank God for blessings
He's sending your way.

Anna M. Matthews

A Lesson Learned

Ever so often we come to dead ends,
And we have to decide what to do,
And even advice from our well-meaning friends
Cannot lessen what we're going through.
Nobody can tell us who's never been there,
Some paths we must walk all alone,
And it is the same most everywhere else,
At least down the roads I have gone.

Once in a while the skies become grey,
With never a hint of the sun,
But I know in my heart there is always a way,
And redemption for everyone.
And however prone we humans can be
For getting our fingers burned,
To give our lives over to God has to be
The most beautiful lesson learned.

Grace E. Easley

*Learn to savor how good the
Lord is; happy are those who
take refuge in Him.*
Psalm 34:9

Small Miracles Everywhere

Every day we see them,
Small miracles everywhere –
Beautiful butterflies dancing in a garden
Where roses blossom fair…
Wee hummingbirds like helicopters
Buzz around aromas sweet,
While in a nearby farmer's field,
A gentle breeze waltzes the golden wheat.
Trees are adorned in an array of leaves –
Oak, maple, elm, and gingko's fan –
While at the beach the waves leap to shore
Discarding seashells on the sand.

The sky is such a powder blue
And each Autumn the geese take wing,
Squawking in a V-formation
Southbound they happily sing.
Stars within the night sky
And the sun, which heats each day,
Are daily miracles oft unnoticed
As we travel on our way.
And don't forget each season –
Spring, Summer, Winter and Fall –
Decked out in their finest array
When they come to call.
Take a few moments to enjoy a sunset
And breathe in some fresh country air,
For every day we can experience them –
Small miracles everywhere!

Linda C. Grazulis

Best Friend

The Lord is my refuge,
My haven of rest.
He shields and protects me
When faced with life's tests.
I go to Him always
In prayer for release.
He never forsakes me
But gives me His peace.
I fret not nor worry,
Burdens are laid at His feet.
I trust and obey Him
Whenever we meet!
Be happy – not dismal,
Be glad and not sad.
The Lord is my keeper,
The best friend I have!

Kathryn Wiesenhoefer

Tiptoe Through the Meadow

Come, tiptoe through the meadow
Where the green, green grasses sway,
Where little bunnies frolic
And turtles wend their way.
Where scattered clover patches
Are fully in their bloom,
And wafting through the meadow
Is a clover-scent perfume.

Come, tiptoe through the meadow
Where the songbirds sweetly sing,
And where in a nearby streamlet
They land to take a drink.
Upon this placid setting
The sun much brighter shines,
So, come tiptoe through the meadow –
'Tis a solace for the mind.

Loise Pinkerton Fritz

*For He is our God; and we are
the people of His pasture, and
the sheep of His hand.*
Psalm 95:7

A Lesson in Song

I'm so very happy today;
I've put my worries on hold.
And there they'll stay, at least for today,
For I found joy untold.

I awoke at dawn in my humble abode
And stretched till my muscles were toned.
Then I took a walk down a country road
As through green fields I roamed.

'Twas there I found such happiness
In a little singing bird;
My heart was truly, truly blessed
At the sweetest song I'd heard.

So, I sang along with this meadowlark;
It taught me a song or two.
It warbles whenever the skies are dark
And when the skies are blue.

I know not what tomorrow may bring;
I've completely dismissed the thought.
I know that today my heart will sing
A song the meadowlark taught.

Lou Ella Cullipher

*I trust in your faithfulness. Grant
my heart joy in your help, That I
may sing of the Lord, "How good
our God has been to me!"*
Psalm 13:6

Someone's in Tears

The sun illuminates the sky,
And flapping wings of birds go by.
The universe declares His glory,
As I sing of redemption's story.
But down the road someone's in tears,
Desperately crying not knowing God hears.
They long for someone to understand
And have lost all hope for a helping hand.
Lord, lead me to that one in despair,
So I can show them how much You care.
Give them strength, God, for their soul.
Oh, lift them up and make them whole.
For all life's answers lie in You –
Wisdom, hope and comfort, too.
Rocky though the road may be,
Sweet solace, Lord, we find in Thee.

Beverly Huff

Kindness From the Heart

Take just a few moments every day
To share some kindness from the heart –
You'll be surprised how uplifted a day
Can be right from the very start.
Send roses to that special someone,
A greeting card can spark a lovely smile.
Visit the lonely, show them you care –
And stay for a little while!
Take time to pray for loved ones
And strangers from afar,
For all have hopes and dreams
And wish upon a star.
A bit of kindness from the heart
Can cheer along life's way –
It's as precious as the sweet aromas
Flowers freely give away.

Linda C. Grazulis

May Your kindness, Lord,
be upon us; we have put
our hope in You.
Psalm 33:22

God's Blessings

Dear God, please bless our family,
And keep us well and strong.
Guide all our many days
As the time quickly passes on.

Give us lots of strength
Going down life's long road
To shoulder all our burdens
And carry all our loads.

When our hearts hang heavy,
Please show us the way,
Past all the gloomy tomorrows
To a bright and sunny new day.

You have blessed us with good times
And a wealth of many friends,
With a happy, caring family
Whose love will never end.

God, thank You for Your blessings,
For hearing all our prayers.
Most of all we thank You
For always being there.

Gloria Swan Kennedy

Be Gracious

Be gracious in your actions,
For people then may see
Your love of God's creations
And pride in being free.
Show kindness to your brothers
So that all men will know
That you respect all others
And love can freely flow.
Be gentle to God's children,
And all of Nature's kin.
Share His love… you'll find it
Gives blessings deep within.

Deborah Beresford

Let Me Live My Life for You

Oh Lord, let me live my life for You
In everything that I say and do.
Please walk with me through dark valleys
And let me soar to life's peaks with You.

Once I thought in yesteryears
That I could manage my life all alone
Only to find my erroneous thoughts
Were not the seeds You had sown.

When life's failures sadden my heart
And I'm filled with great distress,
I reach out to You, dear Savior,
Then I'm filled with much happiness.

May my love for You grow each day,
And please put my doubts to rest,
So that I can live my life for You
And give You my very best.

Shirley Hile Powell

*I will sing to the Lord all
my life; I will sing praise
to my God while I live.*
Psalm 104:33

We Thank Thee,
Lord, for Everything!

We thank Thee, Lord, for bluest skies
That lift our hearts to You.
We thank Thee for Your rainbows, Lord.
Our greatest treasure is You.
We thank Thee for the setting sun
That turns the sky to red
And night that follows when the sun
Silently goes to bed.

We thank Thee for the roses and
For lilies white as snow
And lilacs fragrant in the rain –
You must love them so!
The earth reflects Your mighty hand;
It fills us with thanksgiving.
In praise of You, my heart sings, too,
And time is worth the living.

Margaret Peterson

*Reflect on what I am saying,
for the Lord will give you
understanding in everything.*
2 Timothy 2:7

New Beginnings

Every day is a fresh, new start,
A chance for a new beginning,
To live better than the day before,
A day to keep from sinning.
This day can be a day to spread
God's love and peace around,
To thank Him for a lovely world
Where Nature's gifts abound.
Each day a new experience,
A time to thank and pray,
And to feast upon His mercies
And to make it our best day.

Helen Gleason

God's Domain

Twinkling stars, a silver moon,
Far horizon, sun at noon,
Little streamlet, country lane,
Warmth of Summer, April rain…

Sighing breezes, falling leaves,
Brilliant colors in the trees,
Something lovely, shining hills,
Shadows lengthen, sunshine spills…

Sunrise – sunset, day between,
Nature's bounty, glowing dream,
Love and loving, wondrous gain,
Ours to cherish… God's domain.

Garnett Ann Schultz

Bless the Lord, all creatures,
everywhere in God's domain.
Bless the Lord, my soul!
Psalm 103:22

The Storm Is Over

The storm is over; I made it through –
Shaken, but still standing –
But while in the midst of raging winds,
Life was so demanding.

Quite suddenly I found myself
Lost in angry seas,
So tempest-tossed and all alone,
The worst place I could be.

Then above the storm came Jesus' voice,
"I am the Rock you seek."
I've clung to Him, my stronghold, since
That day I heard Him speak.

Yes, the storm is over – for now,
But I need to stay alert.
Gentle breezes can turn treacherous,
And I can still get hurt.

Thank You, Lord, for raising me up
And keeping me in Your word!
Again clouds are gathering;
Was that thunder that I heard?

Denise A. DeWald

He Is With Me

Because my God is with me,
He will wash away my tears.
He will help me through my sorrows
And conquer all of my fears.
I'll look for a brighter tomorrow
When my day is sad and blue.
I know the sun will shine again
When each day dawns anew.
The faith that God has given to me
Makes me strong in every way.
It carries me through the rough times
And helps me through the day.
I'll praise and glorify my God,
The One who shelters me.
He walks with me through my earthly life
And through all eternity.

Shirley Hile Powell

Faith

I know my heavenly Father
Is ever by my side.
As I travel unknown pathways,
He'll always be my guide.

Although sometimes the twists of fate,
The way ahead obscure,
I know that with my Lord to lead,
My progress will be sure.

When people 'round me prove untrue
Or friends my trust betray,
I turn for solace to my God,
Who hears me when I pray.

When my earthly sojourn ends,
In faith I'll stretch forth my hand,
Knowing that God will take me
Straight to His promised land.

Alice J. Christianson

*Whatever you ask for in prayer
with faith, you will receive.*
Matthew 21:22

My Basket of Blessings

My life, well it's my basket.
Each day the Lord begins
To add His special blessings
As I lift it up to Him.

The blessings of a new day,
The sun, so bright and warm,
That I arose this morning
In a place that I call home…

Flowers in my garden,
Birds that sweetly sing,
Music from my radio –
Oh, what happiness they bring.

106

Hands to help my neighbor,
Work for me to do,
Joy to fill my heart and soul
Whenever I am blue.

My basket's overflowing
At the ending of the day.
Such thankfulness fills my heart…
With such gratitude I pray.

Mary Ann Jameson

Look for the Good
In Those You Meet

I strive to find some special joy
In each and every day –
And try to see only good in those
I meet along the way.

I try to separate good from bad,
Like threshing chaff from wheat –
And leave a bit of newfound hope
In those I've chanced to meet.

For life on earth gets complicated
When we give in to fear –
So, when I meet that one in need,
I offer a listening ear!

Mary S. Chevalier

A True Friend

A true friend offers sound advice
In a tender and loving way.
When others turn away and leave,
A true friend is there to stay.

Someone you can confide in
When your life is in despair,
Whose loving hands uplift you,
In good or bad to share.

There is a special bond of trust
That never fails the test.
No matter what the circumstance,
A true friend gives her best.

For bringing you into my life,
I thank the Lord above,
You have been that one true friend
Who gave unfailing love.

Frances Culp Wolfe

*A faithful friend is a sturdy
shelter; he who finds one
finds a treasure. A faithful
friend is beyond price, no
sum can balance his worth.*
Sirach 6:14-15

The Outdoor Artist

The outdoor Artist pulled out
All the stops today
And set the forest all ablaze
With colorful array.

The hues of yellows, reds and golds,
Of browns and greens and more,
Awaited me at daybreak when
I stepped outside my door.

The greatest outdoor Artist is
The One who made our world.
He decorates the woodland hills
With blissful hues unfurled.

The colors on His palette can't
Be reproduced I'm told.
His vast spectacular collage
In Autumn we behold.

While artists here can never paint
A picture quite as grand,
Let us enjoy each autumntime,
The scenes throughout our land.

Luther Elvis Albright

The Melody in My Heart

There's a melody in my heart,
A song I love to sing;
It tells me of God's goodness
And the happiness it brings.

It sends light to quench the darkness,
To awaken those who sleep.
It gives hope and understanding
And makes my sad heart leap!

Oh, the beautiful harmony stirs me,
Fills my soul with joy and peace.
How I praise my Lord who gave it –
May His love never cease!

Mary S. Chevalier

Seasons Interlude

Leaves are falling one by one,
Autumn's in the air,
Falling softly to the ground –
All within God's care.

Summertime has gone to sleep,
Fall's waiting in the wing
Once again to show her face –
Such a pretty thing.

Wintertime is hiding now
Just around the bend,
Waiting, waiting patiently
With a lovely trend.

Dressed once more in purity
Everything is white.
Seasons of the year behold
Such a pretty sight.

Katherine Smith Matheney

*Cast your care upon the Lord,
who will give you support...*
Psalm 55:23

An Autumn Day

It's a beautiful day for walking
Along the country way;
A beautiful day to revel in
Autumn's grand display.

The hills have changed from Summer's green
To festive colors bold,
And we in awesome wonder see
God's masterpiece unfold.

The tawny fields drowse in the sun,
The harvest gathered in.
Orange-gold pumpkins everywhere
Are heaped high once again.

The little stream meanders on
So peaceful and serene;
It seems to say, "Come rest awhile
From out life's busy scene."

Oak trees have donned their rainbow crowns
To vie for beauty's claim,
While sugar maple trees light up
The nearby country lane.

The sun sinks in a seal of gold,
The vesper hour draws near,
A sacred hush spreads o'er the land
Like no other time of year.

It's a beautiful day for pausing,
To thank our God above,
Creator of the Autumn day
That we so dearly love.

Kay Hoffman

*"Come to Me, all you who
labor and are burdened,
and I will give you rest."*
Matthew 11:28

Morning Prayer

Lord, take my hand in Yours,
Hear me as I pray;
Guide my steps, my heart, my mind
As I travel along life's way.

From deep inside my being,
Hear the words I humbly say;
Give me the strength and hope
To face the dawn of another day.

You are my holy Shepherd,
Within Your fold I long to stay.
As You show me the path to take,
It is Your will I choose to obey.

My heart is filled with happiness;
My spirit is light and gay.
I'm in the shelter of calm waters –
My ship has safely reached the bay.

Eleanor Torchia

He Loves Me Most of All

When I begin to feel alone
Or when the shadows fall,
I talk to Jesus one-on-one;
He loves me most of all.

When trouble knocks upon my door
And tries to stay awhile,
Jesus comes to shelter me;
He brings my heart a smile.

Every time I start to cry
Or feel I can't go on,
Jesus holds me in His arms;
He keeps my spirit strong.

Jill Lemming LeBlanc

We Must Grow in Faith Together

We must never take for granted
The blessings we receive,
As we share the faith within us
With others who believe.

We must grow in faith together
And lift each other up,
As we gather at His table
To share the bread and cup.

We are free to assemble,
To serve and praise the Lord,
And bear witness to all nations
In love and one accord.

We must never be complacent
Or we'll surely drift away
From the fellowship that binds us
When we worship and obey.

We must grow in faith together,
Each one in his own way,
As we gather with God's children
To worship Him and pray.

Clay Harrison

But grow in grace and in the knowledge of
our Lord and Savior Jesus Christ. To Him be
glory now and to the day of eternity.
2 Peter 3:18

Grand Creations

I see the sun, the moon and stars
Created by Your hands.
The planets, all in order,
Move as You command.

I see a tiny snowflake
Or an eagle fly on high.
I watch the mighty ocean waves,
And Summer's blue, blue sky.

For the beauty of the seasons,
For my home and family,
My friends who gather 'round me,
And eyes that I might see.

No other word explains it –
I simply don't know how.
For all Your grand creations, Lord,
I simply shout, "God, wow!"

Mary Ann Jameson

*For You make me jubilant, Lord,
by Your deeds; at the works of
Your hands I shout for joy.*
Psalm 92:5

God Has a Way of Loving

God has a way of loving
When the world seems to pull you down;
His arms will reach out and hug you,
His hands will sorrows unbound.

God has a way of uplifting
A heart that has broken in two.
He'll heal and mend each heartache
With a touch of heavenly glue!

God has a way to comfort
When grief overshadows the way.
He speaks of hope and resurrection
And sends sunshine to brighten each day.

Don't ask me how God does it –
But He'll never let you down.
Just keep focused on His very special love
And you'll be so glad you kept Him around!

God has a way of loving
That's very unique indeed.
You'll never fully understand it –
But just trust Him and you'll see!

Linda C. Grazulis

Let us reach out our hearts
toward God in Heaven!
Lamentations 3:41

123

Peace... Be Still

In this life, no matter what
You might be going through,
Just close your eyes
And let God's peace
Gently come to you.
For God has promised if we ask,
We surely will receive.
Just sit still
And open your heart
And let yourself believe.

Joan Fennell Carringer

I Seek

I seek to know my Savior
More and more each day.
To learn of Him and know Him
In a new and personal way.

I read His word and discover
What He wants me to know,
To live daily by His word,
And He's with me where'er I go.

Thank You, heavenly Father,
For the constant love You give;
I'll cherish it always in my heart
As long as I shall live.

Dona M. Maroney

*For I long to see you, that I may
share with you some spiritual gift
so that you may be strengthened.*
Romans 1:11

Love Will Find a Way

When your hopelessness surrounds you
Like a dark, invading cloud,
When your misery confounds you
And your burdens wear you down...
Even though your heart is aching
With the agony of doubt,
Even though advice you're taking
Is not useful to you now...
Love will find a way.
While a hundred explanations
Can't explain the signs ahead,
While at every destination,
There are none you call a friend...

Even while your problems linger,
Even though you've done your best,
Even while you seek the answers
So your weary soul can rest...
Love will find a way.
Because love has no beginning,
It has been here all along.
Because love has never ended,
Love is never really gone.
So beyond your fear and agony,
Count on love to get you through.
Trust not your own abilities...
God's love, it will find you.

John Frederick Zurn

*In this way the love of God was
revealed to us: God sent His only
Son into the world so that we
might have life through Him.*
1 John 4:9

Faith's Reward

Trees with icy-fingered branches
Wave a greeting as we pass.
Underfoot, a frozen blanket
Crunches where there once was grass.

Winter's breath is frosty white,
A silent cover, chill and deep.
No sound of birds at break of day
To signal time to wake from sleep.

Swirling winds sing lively songs,
Their frigid air sharp as a knife,
And gardens peacefully slumber on
While waiting Spring's warm call to life.

But as for us, we choose to wait
Secure and snug inside our door
While pondering this miracle
Of life to be reborn once more.

Helen M. Motti

Dear God

Dear God
Children's Letters to God

David Heller

ILLUSTRATED BY
John Alcorn

Doubleday
NEW YORK
1987

Library of Congress Cataloging-in-Publication Data
Dear God.
    1. God. 2. Children—Religious life. 3. Imaginary
letters. I. Heller, David.
BT102.D33   1987   231'.0880544   87-8848
ISBN 0-385-24154-2

Dedicated to a God of
Mirth & Kindness:
I Have Faith That YOU
Know How To Take A Joke

Contents

Introduction

When I was five years old or so, there was an afternoon television show called "House Party," which sometimes featured children talking about most anything under the sun. The popular theme of the show, as told and retold by host Art Linkletter, was: "Kids say the darnedest things!" I remember watching the program faithfully. I really liked watching other children on TV, but for all my half decade of life experience I could not figure out what was so funny about them. Now, some twenty-three years later, I believe I understand. Children really tell the truth about life and they do it in a lovable and endearing way. As I have been exploring children's ideas about God and about the world, I have come to realize that kids not only say the "darnedest" things, they say the wisest things as well.

At the same time that I was intrigued with children on television, I was also beginning to learn about religion and my heritage. Growing up in a Jewish family, I was a child surrounded by ritual and history at an early age. Candle lighting was as familiar to me as catching a baseball; prayer was as much a part of my routine as riding a bicycle. But I was also the child of a Holocaust survivor, and this legacy created a special and sometimes formidable challenge for me.

As a child I thought as a child, but I was drawn to the global concerns of adults. I wanted to make sense of how people acted, and I was especially curious about belief and doubt in a God. I asked many questions of nearby grownups, local clergy, and teachers as well as my parents. "Why is the world the way it is?" I asked with tiredless persistence. I received many different answers, as most children do, and I kept searching. A few years later, I became one of the first Jews in a private, Jesuit Catholic high school. This experience, particularly the close relationships I developed with faculty and friends, continued my fascination with the religions of the world. By 1984, after studying psychology and religion at Harvard and Michigan, respectively, the topic of children's God images formally became a part of my life. It was then that I began writing *The Children's God,* a book published in 1986 by the University of Chicago Press.

Writing this book helped me to understand other people's religious views as well as my own. Through my research for the book, I found that children share many ideas about God despite their differences in religion, age, and gender. Most children are concerned with how powerful God is and whether God will be a significant force in their lives. They believe that God is all around, in the sky, in flowers, and in people too. They talk a great deal about "the God in people." These small theologians express clear interest in their spiritual relationship to their neighbors. They seem to conclude that God created the human race with a purpose in mind, and that we are all connected to that purpose and to each other. As twelve-year-old Tamara described, "It's all woven together . . . All of our lives . . . And God is at the center of our world, guiding our destiny."

This book also compelled me to consider more closely my own personality and childhood, as each of my child interviewees opened up to me. I was consistently amazed at how the children's unique personalities influenced their images of God. There are those children who imagine a benign, helping figure—youngsters who picture a "Dr. God, the Therapist." Eight-year-old Mike writes in his letter:

> Dear God,
>   I fell off my bike last week. My leg still hurts a lot. Could you speed up the get well work?
>   Thanks,
>   Mike

There are other children who envision God as a congenial playmate—boys and girls who depict "God, the Friendly Ghost." Seven-year-old Mary provides an illustration:

> Dear God,
>   Thank you for the doll house last Christmas. I wonder if you could stop by to play with me? We could play Family, or School or maybe Bible Stories. Whatever you like.
>   Love,
>   Mary

I find myself learning something new from each of these children, because each of their God images reveals some special quality or outlook. They take me back to a simpler time, yet their interpretations cause me to think a little deeper. Their images remind me that religious belief is indeed a very personal thing and that greater acceptance of religious differences must be a continual pursuit.

While children's ideas about God should be seriously considered, they can also be lightheartedly enjoyed. While I was completing *The Children's God,* I collected a great variety of original drawings, stories, conversations, and letters. I was particularly moved by the children's letters. I also received mail from parents of a variety of religious backgrounds, including devout churchgoers and atheistic parents. They were simply responding to my work with children and wanted to offer a letter or an anecdote. The humor and vitality that leaped forth from so many of their children's original and spontaneous ideas was undeniable. I found myself collecting more letters from other children and sharing the letters with friends and relatives, including my thirteen-year-old and ten-year-old cousins. Adults and children alike seemed to lose themselves in what can only be described as "a childlike sense of wonder and laughter." I knew I must share this colorful parade of letters with a larger audience. One by one, the children's letters provide inspiration for all of us.

Children write to God about all different kinds of things. Full of curiosities, dreams, and stories to tell, children have a wonderful knack for sharing their innermost thoughts in their letters. Some children write at length about everyday concerns—about mom and dad, brothers and sisters, school activities and challenges, and the ups and downs of friendship and play. Family themes are especially vivid since parents play the primary role in helping to develop a child's God image. Some youngsters write to God about the world at large—about international troubles and national leadership, the way men and women act with each other, and those sometimes fuzzy ideas we get from television and movies. Even more than when I was a child in the 1960s, the media seems to have a profound influence on children's notions of good forces and bad forces, heroes and supernatural characters. But some children are even more reflective. They're sincerely curious about really "hard-to-explain" things—like science, nature, and religious belief and doubt. The teachings of the Bible and established religions are frequently apparent in the letters, though these formal influences tend to emerge in humorous and even exaggerated ways. Whatever an individual child's interests, we can be certain that he or she will be quite outspoken and animated—for that is what childhood is all about.

For me, personally, there have been quite a few stops on the journey from curious child to curious interviewer of children. Yet some things have remained the same: Religion conveys for me a great joy and lightness of spirit and children are the ideal messengers of that spirit. They create a house party whenever they speak or write. Their special guests, those characters and images which capture their interest, are limited only by the outer reaches of a child's imagination. As you read on, you will meet some familiar and modern guests like Superman, Mr. T and Ronald Reagan. But you'll also be greeted by some age-old figures like Santa Claus, Moses, and those distant relatives of us all, Adam and Eve. So please join me in enjoying the timeless spirit of children. It is my considerable pleasure to pass along their letters to God and share with you their sweetness.

David Heller

Boston, Massachusetts

---

xiii

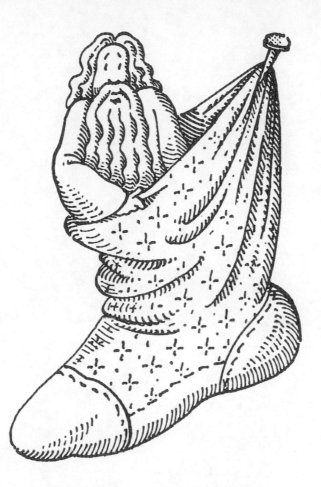

*"Did You Think That
Christmas Would Turn Out
like This When You Started It?"*

Dear God,
Does Pat Robertson really know you personally? If not, I thought you should know that he talks about you a lot.

Your friend,
Brent
[age 8]

Dear God,
Did you think that Christmas would turn out like this when you started it?

Love,
Wendy
[age 7]

Dear God,
Do you have a favorite religion? I'll give you three to choose from—
1. Catholic
2. Lutheran
3. Episcapalin

Best wishes,
Charles
[age 10]

P.S. I'm Episcapalin.

Dear God,
    I think you must be real smart to invent religion. That way you get all the people to look up to you and say your name a lot. I want to be famous too. My names's Frank.

Yours truly,
Frank ✡ ✡ ✡
[age 11]

God,
    What's the story? Why did you make the Jews stay in the desert for 40 years?

Keith
[age 7]

Dear God,
    In school, I drew a picture of Jesus and the 12 disciplens. If you want to see my drawing, stop by my house at 7 tonight.

Love,
Jennifer
[age 9]

Dear God,
   Your my favorite God. I don't have anybody before you. I praise you a lot. I hope you will write me back and think of me always. Call me if you want.
                                        Love,
                                        Jerry
                                        [age 9]

Dear God,
   How old are you? If that Noah story is right, you must be older than my neighbor, Mr. Grubb—and he's really old.
                                        Take it easy,
                                        Tammy
                                        [age 8]

Dear God,
   Can't you make church more fun? What about having a few videos?
                                        Just trying to help,
                                        Celia
                                        [age 10]

Dear God,
   Why did you give Jesus such a hard time? My dad is rough on me too. So I know what it's like. Maybe you both could ease up?

                    Mark
                    [age 11]

Dear Mr. God,
   Do you have a few minutes? I have a few things to say. First, thank you for the bike for Christmas. Second, thanks for the snow. Third, how about more holidays?

                    Sincerly,
                    Angela
                    [age 9]

Dear God,
   I live in a very religious place, but you already no that because you visited. What I want to know is was New York City a mistake? Please tell the truth. We'll keep it a secret.

                    Love,
                    Jamie
                    [age 8]

Dear God,
    Who do *you* pray to? If you don't say prayers, do you think you can let me off the hook?
                                        Jim
                                        [age 9]

Dear God,
    I love you. I just want to let you know ahead of time that I'd like to be there with you in heaven.
                                        Love always,
                                        Sarah
                                        [age 8]

Dear God,
    Why is the cross ✝ the thing you chose for religion?
    We (my friend Jody and me) think you should have tried something different.
    How about something like this? ⬭
                                        Have a nice day,
                                        Pearl
                                        [age 11]
We hope no one has used this before.

Dear God.

If the Lions were as wimpy back in bible times as the ones here are, the Christians would have won.

The Lions are a football team if you did not know it.

I hope that you are not
bothered by this,
Chuck
[age 10]

Dear God,

What religion are the people in London?
Have they got Christianity yet?

Anna
[age 8]

Dear God,

I am a Unitarian. I like this because it is easy to be. We are also Democrats. This is harder to be since Reagan keeps winning.

Love,
Michelle
[age 9]

Dear God,
    I just learned how to spell R E L I G I O N.
I feel good. Now I am learning something else that
we are. It is called P R E S S B U T A R R I U N.
                                    Emily
                                    [age 6]

Dear God,
    How are you doing? I heard that you had a cold. But
keep the faith. We are working on a cure.
                                    Best wishes,
                                    Dr. Tony
                                    [age 11]

Dear God,
    What do you *really* think about atheists? I think that
you must feel like I feel about the Yankees—I hate them.
                                    Tom
                                    [age 9]

Dear God,
    I'd like to make a suggestion, if that's okay. Why
don't you have fewer religions so people would get along
better? We just read about the Crusades a long time ago.
                                    Janet
                                    [age 11]

Dear God,

What do you think about people who convert? My mom says they're stupid. By the way, I like being Jewish.

Love,
Amy
[age 10]

Dear God,

How did you get to know Mary?

Andy
[age 6]

Dear God,

Your burning bush trick is better than Doug Henning. I like your act.

Ron
[age 11]

"Is Jesus Your Oldest Kid?"

Dear God,
My dad get laid off last week at work. Please help him find work quick.
He bugs us a lot when he is home.
Thank you,
Martin
[age 8]

Dear nice god,
I feel close to you. Like you and I are part of the same family.
Maybe we could get married and make it easier.
Your lover,
Tina
[age 7]

Dear God, father of Jesus,
How does it feel to be the biggest, best dad in the whole United States?
You must make out okay on father's day.
Bruce
[age 10]

Dear God,
   My grandma died a year ago. My mom says she is with you. Could you give her this letter?
   Here is the letter:
      Grandma, I'm doing good in school and I met a boy I'm going to marry.
                                    All my love,
                                    Cindy
                                    [age 8]

Dear God,
   Thank you for my parents, my sister Anita, and for my grandma and grandpa. They are all real warm and special. I forgive you for my brother Phil.
   I guess you didn't finish working on him.
                                    Sean
                                    [age 12]

God,
   My father reads to me from your book all the time. I like times when he does.
   The Joseph character is interesting.
                                    Love,
                                    Joe
                                    [age 10]

Dear God,

Do you have an extra plague for my sister. Like you did to the Egyptians.

She's real stupid.

Stanley
[age 8]

Dear God,

Thank you for the nice weather last week. We had some cousins visiting us. They are from Ohio. That is far away.

I wish you could move Ohio closer to us.

Jennifer
[age 7]

Dear God,

My mom is Jewish and my dad is Catholic. My mom says this makes us even more special. Two is better than one.

Do you like to mix things up like this?

See you on all the holidays.

Love you,
Beth
[age 9]

Dear GOD . . .
  Please help my mom and dad not to fight so much.
They act like Marvin Haggler and Larry Holmes.
  They don't even need to wear gloves.
                              Thank you,
                              Will
                              [age 12]

Dear God,
  My dad thinks he is you. Please straighten him out.
                              Wayne
                              [age 11]

Dear God,
  My mom is acting weird because she is getting old.
Can you take back a few gray hairs? That would help
bring the house back to normal.
  Thanks for what you can do.
                              Mike
                              [age 9]

Dear Mr. and Mrs. God,
  What's your family like? Is Jesus the oldest?
                              Karen
                              [age 7]

Dear God, Esq.

My family, the Sandersons, is pleased to invite your family, the Gods, over for bread and wine (I figured you might like this).

You are hereby invited on November the 3, at 7 pm.
Please respond in writing or on a tablet by this date.

Very truly yours,
Sheila Sanderson
Host
[age 11]

Dear God,

Are you in charge of babies?

I have three sisters, which is good. But I would like to put in an order for a brother.

I hope this special order won't upset you.

Love,
Stuart
[age 9]

Dear God,

What is it like at your house? Do you have an address?

My mom says that when you're with God (you), you're always in 7 Heaven.

Is that were I should write to you?

Love and kindness, all
the time
Angela
19 Doe Lane
[age 9]

Dear God,

This is my family.

Now how about a picture of your family?
Brenda
[age 6]

Dear God,

What do you do with families that don't have much faith?

There's a family on the next block like that. I don't want to get them in trouble. I don't want to say who.

See you in church,
Alexis
[age 9]

Dear God,

My Uncle George is from New Jersey. He tells silly jokes and teases me a lot.

I want to ask—are uncles around so that we will like are parents even more?

Your friend,
Scotty
[age 7]

Dear God,

Was there anything special about Bethlehem, or did you just figure that was as good a place as any to start a franchise?

Your friend,
Jim
[age 12]

Dear God,

Was there really a Garden of Eden? My family has a garden too. But it is small and crummy. It just has a few rotten vegetables.

Don't tell my mother I said this please.

Larry
[age 10]

Dear God,

My sister Tina has a girlfriend named Wendy. They are both 15. Wendy has the biggest mouth in the world. No fooling.

It would take a miracle to shut Wendy up. Got any left?

I'm no tattletale,
Tammy
[age 9]

Dear God,

My mom smokes too much. We are all worried about her health. Even the surgeon general. Help her to stop, please.

Why did you make cigarettes anyway? Was that the Devil's work?

Lori Ann
[age 11]

Dear Father of the universe,
Since the whole galaxy is yours you must have a great family barbecue!
Invite me.
Chip
[age 11]

Dear God,
Thank you for giving me to a loving and caring family. That was a choice that was a good one.
By the way as long as I'm writing to you. Was there other families that you tried out first?
Take it easy,
Tito
[age 10]

To God,
If everybody in the whole world is related to everybody else, then how can people get married?
Let's see if you answer that one.
Pia
[age 8]

Dear God,

My mom and my father are divorced. For 3 years.

Nobody's perfect. But why did you pick us? I wish we were all with each other.

Maybe you could have them get along on weekends.

Please,
Stephen
[age 11]

Dear God,

I learned in school that you can make butter flies out of caterpilars. I think that's cool. What can you do for my sister? She's ugly.

Please don't tell my parents I wrote you.

Your buddy,
Greg
[age 11]

*"Do You Spend Your Spear Time
with the Israelites, God?"*

Dear God,
Why can't all the people in the USA for Africa be friends?
A concerned American,
Janet
[age 7]

Holy God,
When someone you know does not have enough money $$$, should you ask him if he needs help? I could not find this in the parables.
Oh it is for pineapple bubble gum.
Love,
Your pal al
[age 9]

God,
I know a kid at school. His name is Tom Chen. He is Chinese. Most of us are not. Boy you like to have variety.
Love,
Andy
[age 10]

Dear God,

Be my friend? It won't cost you nothing and you don't even have to perform too many miracles.

William
[age 8]

Dear God,

I think that you are swell. My priest said that we are wrong if we think that you are only in the clouds. He says you are here on earth too.

If it is okay with my mother, would you like to come over to dinner on Tuesday night?

We are having lasanye!

Hope you can make it,
Madelyn
[age 9]

Dear God,

I feel that Jesus is a friend of mine. Since he's your friend too, that makes us friends. Right or not? Let's get together to play sometime. You can bring all the toys you have and I'll bring mine. We'll see who has more.

Love,
Lori
[age 7]

Dear God,

On earth as it is in heaven. You and my friend Cindy are the best.

> Love,
> Carol
> [age 10]

Dear God. God of Justice.

I hate to bother you but there's this kid. His name is Billy Forte. He's always bothering me and being mean. He tried to steal my glove. Can you rub him out!!!

> Sorry to bug you,
> John
> [age 8]

Dear God,

My girlfriends and I started the God Fan Club. Would you like to buy a button? We're going to make them ourselves.

Just so you know, here are the members so far.

Tracy, Mary, Me, Lynn, Paula, and You

> Love, Sue
> [age 8]

Dear God,
I live in Maine. I have a lot of friends here. People here are great.

Some people say we talk funny. That makes me mad. They should talk. They are from Boston.

Love,
Amanda
[age 8]

My mother's friends live in Boston.

Long Distance to GOD:
I hope that you are well . . .

And taking care of the world. Please make us friendly with all the Arabs, with the eastern peoples and with the Africaners.

And please, this is important. Make me friends with Johnny Martins. We do not get along.

Alphonse
[age 10]

Dear God,
O hello God. I love music and so do my friends. We sing in the church choir together. Please make sure we always stay friends. Help us to sing better.

Judith
[age 11]

Dear God,

Why couldn't anyone in Israel get along in the Bible? There was always stone throwing and fighting. Jake, Joseph, Abe, Moses—you name them. No person was the friend of another. That's no good.

Roy
[age 10]

Dear God,

My baseball team went 5 and 15 last year. That means we lost 15 times. I hurt a lot about this. Please say a prayer for us.

Thanks,
Kevin
[age 9]

My friend Sam is on the team too. He's nice but he strikes out a lot.

Dear God old pal,

How's it going man? Can you fix it so my friends and me can stay out later in the summer.

We are cool.

Mark
[age 11]

Dear God,

Who was Mohammed? Was he a friend of yours like Jesus?

Also, were Moses and Joshua friends or just business partners?

> I'm taking a class on
> religions,
> Fanny
> [age 12]

Dear Gods,

All the kids on my block have 3 Speeds. You wouldn't want me to be left out . . . So

> Merry Christmas ahead of
> time,
> Bob
> [age 9]

Dear God,

Did you ever play 4 Squares with the other gods in heaven. We play it here on my block.

Maybe you play 4 Halos or something.

> Love and kisses,
> Dana
> [age 8]

Dear God,
I am having fun and making friends. Dave is talking to me about things you do and say. But I told him. How should I know? Ask my friend George. He gets A's in school and I get C's!

Sorry,
Joe
[age 9]

Dear God,
You are a good friend to me when I am in need. Like maybe now. I am broke.

Your buddy,
Howard
[age 12]

Dear God,
Best regards. I am going to go play with my girl-friends after this. I am going to tell them about the stuff I just talked about and about the banner and pencils that the man gave me.
If you told him what to buy for the kids, thank you. You have good taste.

Heather
[age 9]

Dear God,

I found out that I have to get glasses. I am worried about what my friends will say. They may tease me and say 4 eyes. Please make sure they do not.

I am not vain or anything.

Carmen
[age 9]

Dear friendly God,

I think you are like a regular person.

I do not believe those people who say you are dead or far away.

You probabaly live on the next street.

Marcy,
[age 8]

Dear God,

I want to know if you like these men.

Jerry Fallwall
Jesse Jackson
Ron Reagan
Pat Boone
Frank Sunatro

They are supposed to be religious I think. So I thought you know them maybe.

Stewart
[age 12]

Dear God,
    I just made a new friend today.
    His name is Dave Heller. He is white and I am black
    but that is fine.
    We both love basketball.
                    Love,
                    Bill the thrill
                    [age 9]

Jesus,
    You and me is tight.
                    I luv you,
                    Richard
                    [age 6]

To God,
    Who do you spend your spear time with?
    The Israelites?
                    Ken
                    [age 12]

"Do You Watch All of Us People
on a Big TV Screen?"

Dear GOD,
    I think there is much too many things about money
these days. Especially on television.
    You should take some money away from people so it
would not be such a big deal.
                            Don't tell them
                            who gave you the idea,
                            Susie
                            [age 7]

Dear God,
    Do you watch television?
    Or do you just see Earth on a big screen?
    Do you have a channel for Forest Hills in New York?
That is where I live.
                            Let me know when you
                            will be watching so that I
                            can dress up,
                            Sybil
                            [age 11]

Dear God,
    Channel 4 has a nice peacock on its ads. I bet you
watch them. Peacocks are in the bible, my minister says.
                            Take it slow,
                            Dennis
                            [age 9]

Dear God,

I see President Reagan on TV all the time. He is always waving and smiling.

You should get your own station too. That way every person will know who you are and what you look like. Just like President Reagan.

I say good prayers,
Marianne
[age 9]

Dear God,

You, Michael J. Fox, and Webster are my favorite stars. But why did you make Webster so short?

Marissa
[age 10]

Dear God,

You must be very big. Like William the Refrigerator Perry.

Love,
Mary
[age 9]

Dear God,
   Do your kids watch cartoons on Saturdays? Or are they helping you get ready for church on Sunday?
                              Your friend,
                              Ted
                              [age 7]

Dear God,
   What's your best sport? Mine is basketball. I like the Pistons. I guess you don't, since they don't win much. Do you get ESPN?
                              Tim
                              [age 11]

Hey, God,
   Do you know how in commercials they say they are going to take a break to bring us a word from the sponsor?
   Well you should do that with people in their homes because you are everybody's sponsor. That would be neat. That way you could comunicate with the people.
                              Stay Cool,
                              Riley
                              [age 12]

Dear God,
Did you make any money on the movie, Oh God Book II?

> Just kidding,
> Jerome
> [age 12]

Dear God,
My mom always says that my brother and me would like to stay up so late that we may as well stay up for Sermonette.

She says it is a religious show. Are you the host? Are you like David Letterman?

> What time are you on,
> Risa
> [age 8]

Dear God,
What is your top magazine if you read them?
I think they are all sleazy, besides Seventeen.
Maybe you like Time. My dad reads that and, besides, you created time so they got the idea from you.

> Love,
> Louise
> [age 11]

Dear God,
 Is Krypton a real place?
 Maybe it is just a place in Hollywood.
        Frank
        [age 9]

Dear God,
 What do you think about all those movies about you around Easter time? I think they're kind of corny, myself.
        Your buddy,
        Charles
        [age 9]

Dear God,
 Is Mr. T on your side or the other side?
        Love,
        Hank
        [age 10]

Dear God,
 Can't you do something about all the bad news on TV? I always change the chanell.
        Cindy
        [age 7]

Dear God,
   "Highway to Heaven" is my favorite show. Do you help write it?
                                        Love,
                                        Alice
                                        [age 9]

Dear God,
   I wonder if you could help me out. My mom and dad said I can't watch TV for a week. So I guess I'm going to miss all those religious shows, unless you do something. How about putting in a good word for me?
                                        Love,
                                        Matt
                                        [age 7]

Dear God,
   I think the "Today" show is corny. I watch it sometimes before I catch the bus to school.
   You should do the "Tomorrow" show. It would be good because you know the future. All the people would watch. I bet your ratings would be out of this world.
                                        Best wishes,
                                        Roger
                                        [age 11]

Dear God,
Did you see "The Karate Kid"? You really should, too. You could learn alot about life.

I love movies,
Candace
[age 10]

Dear God,
They could have more bible stories on TV. I recommend the King Solomon story, Moses, Jesus, and the lady who turned into salt.
The Flood might make it difficult. It would be hard to show and the kids might not watch. Plus there would not be enough parts for people. Just animals.

With love,
Roberto
[age 9]

Dear God,
What is your opinion of Marie Osmond? Do you like her better because she comes from a religion?

I want to be a singer too.
I am a Catholic.
Lisa
[age 9]

Dear God,
　　Thank you for Rob Lowe. Yea. We love him. He is the best thing on earth.

　　　　　　　　　　　　Cindy and Laura
　　　　　　　　　　　　[age 12]

Dear God,
　　What do you get paid? My dad says the guy who reads the news on Channel 2 (CBS) gets paid more than you.
　　Why don't they give you a big raise?
　　　　　　　　　　　　I care,
　　　　　　　　　　　　Jamie
　　　　　　　　　　　　[age 11]

Dear God,
　　Do you and Mr. Rogers talk to each other. He is very wise.

　　　　　　　　　　　　Love,
　　　　　　　　　　　　Anthony
　　　　　　　　　　　　[age 6]

Dear God,

What do you think about the Olympics? Don't you think all the countries should go? When they are on TV I watch all of them. Even the dancing and the speeches.

Try to watch the next one. You might like it. It will be in a place called Soul in 1988.

Love,
Jack
[age 12]

Dear God,

A lot of folks say there is too much rough stuff on TV and too much killing too.

I say there is too much rough and tough stuff and killing in the Bible.

Make my day,
Derek
[age 11]

Dear God,

I was watching TV when the Challenger shuttle exploded. That was a sad thing.

Was there anything that you could have done? Were you mad because they came too close to your territory?

We're sorry,
Jose
[age 11]

"There Isn't Any School in Heaven, Is There?"

Dear Jesus,
How did you learn all that stuff in the Book by Luke without going to school much?

Sharon
[age 7]

Dear God,
I read about Abraham in school. Why did you give him such a hard time before you let him become a teacher?
The teachers here got it easy.

Barry
[age 9

Dear God,
You don't have to spell real good to get into heaven, do you?
My teacher told us that when we meet St. Peter we have to spell a word like exagarate. If you get it right, you go to heaven. If you're wrong, you go down stairs.
I don't mean the principils office.

Sincerly,
Dom
[age 10]

Dear God,
 I am a Christian Scientist person. In school I am in the third grade. We learn about many religions but not ours. Are you prejudiced or something?
                    I want to know,
                    Alicia
                    [age 9]

Dear New Testament God,
 Since you like to write so much, maybe you could write my current events term paper for me. It could be about anything—even you!
                    I am desparate,
                    Raymond
                    [age 12]

Dear God,
 The World Series starts on Tuesday. School is in the way. One of them has to go.
 I vote school. Can you make it snow even if it is the start of October?
                    Good luck Tigers,
                    Pete
                    [age 10]

Dear God,

Did you invent math to count the animals on Noah's ark? Do we still need it?

Jeanne
[age 11]

Dear God,

Help. I have a favor to ask you. Mr. Arene teaches us. He is pretty strictly mean. I think he does not go to church either.

I wonder if you could send Jesus or an angel down to talk with him. Maybe I could invite Jesus in for my history project. That way Mr. Arene won't expect anything.

End of letter,
Orson
[age 12]

Dear God,

My people believe in Islam. Most of the other people at school do not. I live in Masachusetts.

Can you put more Islamic people in schools and houses in Masachusetts.

Thank you,
Ahmed
[age 12]

Dear God,
Hi from School. No message.
Love,
Carla
[age 6]

Dear God.
I just moved to a new school. We used to live in North Carolina. People talked about you a lot there. Now we live in a place called Santa Monica. The school here is different. Real different. My dad says the kids here are sun worshippers.
Love,
Kendra
[age 12]

Dear God,
My mom says that I can only stay out after school till it gets dark.
My question is: Can you make the sun stand still?
I figured if you did it once you could probaly do it again.
Freddie
[age 11]

Dear God,
Did Matthew and John have to go to college?
Back here in grade 4,
Art
[age 10]

Dear God,
I love school and I try my best all the time. I also say my prayers every night.
I hope this counts when it's my turn to be judged.
A good Christian,
Gloria
[age 11]

God and who all is listening,
MAKE SCHOOL ONLY AN HOUR A DAY!
A good student
[age 7]

Dear God,
Did you make pencils and pens just like you made men and girls.
I think pencils and pens go together better.
Your friend,
Charles
[age 12]

Dear heavenly father, (God)
I pray to you each and every night. Sometimes I pray to you during Science—this is not good for my grades.
Davida
[age 11]

Dear God,
Are Hebrew schools better than regular schools?? I know that you must be Jewish, but try to be honest.
Hello,
Linda
[age 8]

Dear God,
I hate gym. I bet Sarah and Rachel and Becky did not have to do gym stuff in the Bible.
Boy those were the days.
Love and prayers,
Naomi
[age 10]

Dear God,
When you threw Adam and Eve and all the others out of the garden, that must be when you started to have schools. You must have been plenty mad.

Hope this gives you a
laugh,
David
[age 9]

Dear God,
My dad is a professor in college. They have all the knowledge in the world there.
If you are in Michigan, its ok if you use the library.

Working hard,
Sally
[age 8]

Dear sweet and friend God,
I am being very good. I am good to my mom, my dad, my brother Bill, and my sister Elizebeth. I am nice to my friends like you. I am nice to my grandma and grandpa too.
I am *even* nice to my teachers. I try to forgiving them for being so boring.

Love,
Kristen
[age 8]

Dear God,

I am going to begin junior high next year. You helped me make it so far. Do not leave me now!

Please,
Les
[age 12]

Dear God,

I would like to know if you are like the principle of a school and all the presidents and kings are like teachers.

Andrea
[age 7]

To my God,

I have a drawing for you.

This is my school.   This is a baseball diamond.

The school is there now. I go every day. The base-ball diamond is where you play baseball. It is not there yet. All we need is a little help in building it.

> Let us know if you can
> help,
> Anthony
> [age 11]

Dear God,
I am doing police for you.
My english teacher, Mrs. Clayburn, has pointed ears.
I think she is Satin.

> Keep me covered,
> George
> [age 8]

Dear God,
We read that you made a bush burn to the ground and you did not use matches. Wow. I would like to see this done to my school.

> Yea,
> Timmy
> [age 10]

GOD
1 NORTH POLE
EARTH 7777
How is it up there where you are?
I learned about you in geography. Say hi to Santa
Claus.

Bea
[age 9]

Dear God,
We learn about you a lot in Sunday school. We heard
that you don't like temples with money in it and that you
don't like Romans much either.
Who do you like?

Signed Bill,
I am easy to like
[age 10]

Dear God,
How far did you get in school?
I stayed back last year and I am worried.

Tyler
[age 10]

Dear God,

Thank you for helping the poor people all around the world and for helping to educate them too.

That must be hard work. Do your kids help or are they too busy doing they're homework?

Love,
Cherie

Dear God,

Do you have schools in heaven or are the angels and servants born smart?

Doris
[age 11]

"Is There a Special Place in Heaven for Cabbage Patch Kids?"

Dear God,
    Hockey is pretty tough but I love it.
    I always say a prayer for all the players' injuries after the games.
                    Kevin
                  [age 12]

Jesus,
    I feel very near to you.
    I feel like you are beside me all the time.
    Please be with me on Thursday. I am running in a 3 mile race then. I will need all the speed in the world. If you are not busy with other things, maybe you could be at the starting line, the finish line, and everywhere in between.
                  Frankie
                  [age 11]

Dear God,
    Were you a BOY Scout? I am.
    Did you ever camp out in the desert and play jokes on people in the Bible? I bet you did.
    We do all the time and have a blast.
                  Nat the rat
                  [age 10]

Dear God,

I am fond of you. No question about it.

I love to cook. Today, I would like to make something for You. How about an omelette with bread and butter. I'll put lots of cheese in it.

Do you eat bacon? I don't know since I am a Christian. You might be kosher or something.

Love,
Melissa Sue
[age 11]

Dear Dear Dear God,

I see you in my dreams all the time.

I know it is you because you have a crown on and you are always fishing.

Say hello next time.

Love,
Craig
[age 9]

Dear God,

If you think it was cool the way Jesus walked on the water, you should watch me water ski!

Steve
[age 12]

Dear Jesus,

Since you retired two thousands years ago what kinds of things do you do?

Maybe you should try bowling or you could sing in a church group like my grandmother does.

Your friend,
Pam
[age 9]

Dear God,

My mom tells me a story about you every night. Last night she told me about how you always remember your mother on her birthday. And you give her divine gifts.

I think she was kidding me and herself.

Love,
Holden
[age 7]

Dear God,

Do you have toy spaceships and things like that? That must be fun, but hard to keep track of.

You should always put your toys away when you are done.

Randy
[age 8]

Dear God, of Bible fame,

Do you know me? I carry an American Express card. Just kidding. Guess what. I'm going on a trip to California next month.

I guess you know that already.

> Hope your miracles are
> good ones,
> Ernie
> [age 11]

Dear God,

Was building car models big when you were a kid? Or whatever they called you.

> Warren
> [age 7]

Dear God,

I bet you will never guess what this is.

> Love,
> Sandy
> [age 10]

P.P.S.

It's a machine that makes Christmas presents. Do you think you can top it? How bout this year?

Dear God

Do you have a special place for Cabbage Patch kids in heaven? Are they closer to you because they come from nature?

Love,
Angela
[age 8]

Dear God,

I like to read a lot. We read *The Great Gatsby* in school. Do you have time to read? I bet you like religious books and biographies.

Please write me back,
Terry
[age 12]

Dear God,

I have a big collection of dolls. Sometimes I play Bible with them. I have them act your stories. Once I had them do the ten plagues. Then I had them go in the desert. I was not too rough on them.

Hi,
Charlotte
[age 9]

Dear God,

Do you like the Montreal Canadians? Are you just an American God? I like them even though they are French.

Your buddy,
Dan
[age 9]

Dear God,

Do you ever get bored? I do. Do you get into trouble then? Is that why you started thunder and rain?

Let me know,
Paula
[age 11]

Dear God,

Thanks for the Air Jordans for Christmas. You must be a basketball fan like me. What do you wear, Air Moses? We have a Moses here too, but he's big and he plays for the NBA!

Your humble star,
Ron
[age 12]

Dear God,
   Want to hear a joke? What is red, very long, and you hear it right before you go to sleep? Give up? Answer is a *sermon.*

                         Your friend,
                         Frank
                         [age 11]

Dear God,
   I just learned how to play chess. Does the earth look like a chessboard to you?
                         Libby
                         [age 11]

God,
   I need to confess. I am sorry but I looked at my older brother Eddie's *Playboy* magazine. I didn't really like it though.
                         Sorry,
                         George
                         [age 10]
God, when do you think it would be okay to start going out with girls?

Dear God,

What do you think of Hulk Hogan? Wrestling is fake. Isn't it?

Thanks for the inside
story,
Carol
[age 8]

Dear God,

I just want to say hi! And thanks for all the people you are helping who are starving.

I'm okay here. But there is one thing. I love tennis very much and it is hard to get a court around here. Can you build some more in my neighborhood?

Thank you,
Erica
[age 8]

Dear God,

When I get to high school I want to be captain of the cheerleaders. Please help me make the team.

You would like the school. It's Catholic.

Mary Ellen,
[age 12]

Dear God,

I wonder if we have a lot in common. Do you like the Beach Boys? I do. I live near the Pacific Ocean.

From the west coast,
Amanda
[age 10]

Dear God,

Art is my favorite subject. I want to draw you a picture of you. Here goes.

I need to work on details. It would help if you could come down so that I could get a look at you.

Michael
[age 7]

Dear God,

I love to eat. Thanks for all the food. Pizza was the best idea you had.

Ralph
[age 7]

"What Did Adam and Eve Do for Fun?

Dear God,

What is the rest of the story about when you made boys and girls? There must be a reason why you made two different brands of people.

Hank
[age 6]

Dear God,

My daddy says you must have a good sense of humor. That's why you created Joan Rivers and Boy George.

Love,
Ellen
[age 9]

Dear God,

When do you think it's okay to start dating? How old were you when you went out with Mrs. God? Did you kiss her on the first date?

Your friend,
Cheryl
[age 10]

Dear God,

Do you think there's enough love these days? I feel there's a shortage.

Love,
Ken
[age 9]

Dear God,

I have a crush on a boy in my class (third grade). His name is Ralph. Do you know him? I'm a little scared. So I wonder if you could do a check on him.

Best regards,
Ellen
[age 9]

Dear God,

I go to a Catholic school. The priests there are very nice. But did you ever think of giving these men different clothes. I think the nuns can stay the same.

Curious,
Mary Jo
[age 10]

Dear God,
    How involved do you get in marriages? Do you give the couples any time alone?

                    Just asking,
                    Wayne
                    [age 12]

Dear God,
    I went to my cousin's wedding last week. I heard that you were there. I must have missed you. Do you get to all the weddings or do you just pick some? You must eat a lot of cake.

                    Love,
                    Alexandria
                    [age 10]

God,
    I am a nice girl. I am glad I am not a boy. They are ugly. Only Jesus was nice.

                    Love,
                    Andrea
                    [age 6]

Dear God,
   You and Brooke Shields are my two favorite people who are older than I am.
                    Love,
                    Joanne
                    [age 11]

Dear God,
   What do you think of people who act sexy? I think they are kidding themselves. It is better to act like you really are.
   I try to act religious. I do my best.
                    Trying hard,
                    Brandon
                    [age 9]

Dear God,
   When you made love was it hard to plan?
   Is that why girls and guys act so goofy when they go out?
                    With many times love,
                    Brett
                    [age 9]

Dear God,
   I read about Miriam and Moses. Boy she was a good sister to him.
   I hope that he appreciated her. Some men don't.
                              Amy
                              [age 10]

Dear God,
   I'm writing to complain about how men get the biggest say in everything. I want this to stop. Now.
   I want to be President some day and things are going to change. We're going to need a tornado or a hurricane or something.
                              I will let you know,
                              Linda
                              [age 11]

Dear God,
   Why do boys like dirt so much? I think it might have been better if you got the people out of the desert sooner.
                              Candy
                              [age 8]

Dear God,

Do women in heaven dress up and wear makeup or are they just down to earth people?

I'd like to know,
Wendy
[age 10]

Dear God,

Why do men and girls always fight? Did you believe that the earth would be more interesting that way?

John
[age 8]

Dear God,

When Jonah was in the whale was it a he whale or a she whale. I think girls are probably fatter.

Mike
[age 7]

Dear God,

I'm glad that you are a man. If you were not, you might not have made boys.

I am a boy,
Darren
[age 10]

Dear God,
I think if you were a woman you would be more involved with domestic things like cooking and cleaning. And sewing.

Karen Ann
[age 9]

Dear God,
I read about how Delilah cut Samson's hair. Is that why there are so many female hairdressers?

Warren
[age 10]

God,
What did Adam and Eve do for fun? My mom said they played with toys and ate but I know better.

Chris
[age 9]

Dear God,
Girls are weird. Except for my mom.

Love you,
Timmy
[age 7]

Dear God,

Why do we always have to let the girls go first? I bet they did not want to go first when the Christians were killed in the stadiums.

Carl

[age 10]

Dear God,

When you were small, did you always listen to your mom? Women think they know everything but they do not.

I bet if you listened you would not be so big and powerful today. That is a fact.

Hello God,

Bryn

[age 9]

Dear Ms. God:

I believe that you are a woman. In fact I am sure for sure. I think that is why the rivers and sky and birds are so beautiful.

If by some flook you are a boy please do not take it out on me. Boys should not hit girls.

Trisha

[age 11]

"Volcanos Are Cool, But You Should Watch Your Temper, God!"

Dear God,

Do angels do carpentry and plumbing in the sky? If you don't have to be too handy, I would like to apply.

Yours,
Carmen
[age 8]

To the Lord,

I don't buy that evolution stuff.
I think that you did the whole thing by yourself.

Scott
[age 9]

Dear God,

I used to want to be an astronaut. But I'm not sure it's safe anymore. What's the weather report?

Kevin
[age 12]

Dear God,

I think that you are wonderful. When you invented snow, did you know that people would use it for skiing?

Love,
Amy
[age 10]

Dear God,
     Next time you send a flood, could you please send
me a telegram beforehand? Mostly, I've been good.
                         Waiting to hear,
                         Ted
                         [age 12]

Dear God,
     Do you have a giant computer or do you count all
the people of the world on your fingers?
                         Love,
                         William
                         [age 6]

Dear God,
     I am a big fan of yours and Einstein's, God.
     I think that you are both very smart.
     But he made bombs and you try to stop them.
     That is better.
                         Jan
                         [age 10]

Dear God,

Why didn't you make cars earlier, God? That way the Jews could have good speed and gotten away from the Egyptians' land faster and David could have made a clean get away from Goliath.

Your friend,
Theresa
[age 9]

Dear God,

When you had birds fly south for winter did you think people would too?

We are going to Florida for February vacation!

Love,
Patricia
[age 10]

Dear God,

Do you feel that the scientists and the presidents are to blame for nuclear weapons or are you willing to take on the responsability your self?

Jerome
[age 12]

Mr. God,

I think it is amazing the way everything fits together in the world. Look at heat in our houses, the moon, the sun and rain so farmers' plants will grow.

How do you do it? Mirrors?

Judy,
[age 11]

Dear God,

Volcanos are cool. But you should learn to control your temper (that is what my mother always says to me).

Love,
Victor
[age 11]

Dear God,

I learned that when it is 1 o'clock here it is a different time in China. Why? Did you want to keep us guessing?

Sincerely,
Ellen
[age 9]

God,

Is a hail storm a big God sneeze? Bless you.

Terrence
[age 8]

Dear God,
 Thank you for all the great food that we can grow.
 My two favorite foods are watermelon and ice cream (rocky road).
 It would be great if by 2000, we could grow ice cream (at least vanilla, chocolate, and rocky road).
 If you are planning on making some changes that would be a good one.
                         Love,
                         Mel
                         [age 10]

Dear God in the heavens,
 I am flying to New Orleans next week with my family. We are going to something called Marti Gras.
 I will look for you on the way.
                         Love always,
                         Sharona
                         [age 9]

Dear God,
 Did you make it so cold in Michigan because you thought we could take it? Or was it a practical joke of yours?
                         I ain't laughin,
                         Eric!
                         [age 11]

GOD
God's Lab
Earth to God. Earth to God. Come in God.
POW. POW.
Hey God. Let's play making things. Let's make a radar station. Then let's make a new kind of plane. It will have supersonic hearing. That way it can catch hijackers. They will have to report to the devil then.
                                        Tim
                                        [age 10]

Dear God,
    I live in Michigan. I heard a song that says it don't rain in a place called Indianapolis. I heard that it isn't far away. Why don't you let it rain there?
                                        Tim
                                        [age 7]

Dear God,
    What I want to know is—where do people go when they die? My dad says you go to Russia if you're not good. I don't think so because it's too cold there.
                                        Yours truly,
                                        Andrew
                                        [age 9]

Dear God,

I think it's unbelievable the way you made thunder and lightning bolts. We like the way you make lightning bolts so much, we put them on our football uniforms! I play for the Chargers.

Dan
[age 11]

Dear God,

I'm in the fifth grade and we have to do a science fair project. We can get help from a grownup (honest). I think maybe you would be ok. Can you help me out?

Help,
Diane
[age 11]

Dear God,

I heard that you can predict the future. Are you better than a horoscope? What do you think I'm going to ask for next Christmas?

Best wishes,
Susan
[age 11]

Dear God,
   I love you. I love the way you made the sky and the
sun.
   One thing I wondered though. Doesn't it get kind of
hot up there near the sun?
   We are air conditioned so we are O K.
                              Love,
                              Deirdre
                              [age 8]

To God,
   My question is this one. Did you create all the oceans
at once or add when you needed it?
   Was the Pacific hard to do?
                              Ronny
                              [age 8]

Dear God,
   Have you ever wondered if you made a mistake?
   Do you think may be it would have been better to do
babies different?
   I mean look at all the trouble it has made.
                              Let me Know,
                              Leon
                              [age 12]

*"Is That Khadafy Guy
like Pharoah in the Bible?"*

Dear God,
   I am Jewish and I have visited the state of Israel three times.
   My dad says that Jews and Arabs are cousins.
   I have a question for you.
   If Jews and Arabs are supposed to be cousins, how come they can't get along?
   I get along better with my cousin Riva better than that.
                              Love,
                              Sylvia
                              [age 9]

Dear Mr. God,
   Why don't you have girls fight in wars? Even in the Bible they didn't. You'd think that because they are hard to get along with, they would be good at fighting!
                              Just an idea,
                              Marty
                              [age 10]

Dear God,
   I thought Rambo was dumb. Please stop the wars so we don't have any more of this.
                              Curt
                              [age 8]

Dear God,
    Are counrty is trying bad to be good. We invaded
Grenade and Libbya to keep the peace.
    You would be proud.

                                Born in the USA,
                                Tommy
                                [age 9]

Dear God,
    I want to suggest a thing.
                                More Peace!
    While I have your atention, I would also like to ask
for a pair of Reebok sneakers for Christmas.

                                Thank you, I love you,
                                Caroline
                                [age 11]

Dear GOD,
    Please help the Democats and the Republicans to
get along. That way we could get along with other places
too. Like Russia and the Arabs and the Vietnams.

                                Thanks,
                                Clark
                                [age 10]

Dear God,
Please make all the people on the earth better to each other. That means no more terrorism and violence like on tv.
I want to say thanks for that you are trying to do.
Best wishes,
Anita
[age 11]

Dear God,
Why did you make it so there is always to sides to things, good guys and bad guys, east and west? We are all the same. Aren't we?
Truly,
Ken
[age 12]

Dear God,
I read in the paper about the summit with the Russians.
Is that anything like the summit in Houston?
Bill
[age 9]

Dear God,
    When I grow up will I have to fight in the army? Will there be a war?
    I'm not chicken or anything. I just want to know in advance.
                                    Terry
                                    [age 10]

Dear God,
    I think the Ayatolah is crazy. My family moved from Iran to America. We like it here.
    The Ayotolah belongs in a funny farm—that is what the Americans call it. My dad says that to. Do you agree?
                                    I'm being good,
                                    Paul
                                    [age 9]

Dear God,
    I think President Regan is doing a good job. But he is getting too old. Can you make him live longer?
                                    Bless you,
                                    Celia
                                    [age 12]

Dear God,
    If Jesus was alive today what country would you send
him to? I recommend the US of A. We really need him.
                        Love,
                        Edward, Jr.
                        [age 11]

Dear God,
    Was there a China in your day? Did you know Mar-
cus Polo?
                        Ted
                        [age 8]

Dear God,
    I read about what the Turks did to the Armenians a
long time ago. That wasn't nice. I'm Armenian.
                        Garo
                        [age 8]

Dear God,
    Do you try to avoid Russia when you travel?
                        Love,
                        Sharon
                        [age 7]

Dear God,
    Is that Khadafy guy like Pharoah in the Bible or is he worst?
                        Your fan,
                        Alex
                        [age 8]

Dear God,
    I think that President Reagan is like my grandfather but my grandfather is nicer. Did you vote for Reagan?
                        Love,
                        John
                        [age 7]

Dear God,
    My family and me went to Germany last summer. We stopped at those camp places were a lot of people died.
    My question is—did you know about this? Were you away then?
                        Please answer when you can,
                        Cindy Ellen
                        [age 11]

Dear God,
   The bomb is not such a hot invention. Maybe you should recall it.
                              Love,
                              Margaret
                              [age 12]

Dear God,
   My family and I are practicing Catholics. The stuff in North Ireland bothers us a lot. I don't know if your Irish or not. Maybe you could help though.
                              Sincerely,
                              Kathleen
                              [age 10]

Dear General God,
   Boy, you sure do have a lot of wars here. We learned in history about World Wars I and II. Then there was the korean war. I don't know much about that. Then there was Vietnam. Now there always seem to be some fighting going on.
   I figure we must be sergeants to you. You must want things this way. Otherwise it would not have been like that in the Bible too. And there was plenty of WAR there too.
                              Andy
                              [age 10]

Dear God,
 That was a cool trick with the slingshot.
       Dave
       [age 10]

Dear God,
 Could you talk to the Sihks and Hindus. I am Hindu but I live in America. I have family far away. I don't want to see them harmed.
 In case you don't know, America is not too far from Canada.
       With love and
       kindness,
       Mahua
       [age 9]

Dear God,
 I saw a poster in a store that went like this:
WAR IS BAD FOR KIDS AND OTHER LIVING THINGS LIKE THAT
 As a kid i feel it is my duty to tell you about this. If you have not seen it you should. You can get it at Woolworth's.
       One of the kids,
       Sandy
       [age 10]

Dear Jesus,
    Are we related?
    My two uncles have beards. Maybe we are. (They are
in the army though.)
                        Love,
                        Francine
                        [age 7]

Dear God,
    Whose side were you on in the civil war?
    Please tell me the truth. I live in South Carolina.
                        Gretchen
                        [age 8]

Dear God,
    At church my minister talks a lot about throwing
stones and sins. Any idea what he means?
    I think you must know. I don't get the hang of this
stuff.
                        A regular church-goer,
                        Artie
                        [age 11]

*"Is There a Christmas
in Russia, God?"*

Dear God, Jesus, Mary, or who ever is there,
    I have always wondered. Do people in far off places like Syria and Arabia have Christmas?
    If they do not what do they think they are doing when they eat turkey and stuffing and sing carols.
                                    Happy New Years,
                                    Troy
                                    [age 7]

Dear God,
    What do bunnies have to do with Easter?
    Why don't you have camels instead?
                        I will let you know if I
                        think of anything else to
                        do.
                        Brian
                        [age 10]

Dear Santa,
    I was going to write God but I heard that you were in charge of toys.
                        Love ♡ ♡ ♡
                        Brooke
                        [age 6]

Dear God,
    We learned in school about a book called the koran.
Do they do that one at Easter Vigil or something?
                                    I am curious,
                                    Charlotte
                                    [age 12]

Dear God,
    Do you have a Christmas tree or a whole (maybe
holy) forest? It must be hard to light it all up.
                                    Danny
                                    [age 9]

Dear Jesus,
    I want to thank you for going up there on the Cross
for us every Good Fridays.
    You must be real happy when the weekend is over.
                                    Thanks,
                                    Anita
                                    [age 11]

Dear God,
    Easter is eggsactly what I would have created.
                                    Loren
                                    [age 11]

Dear God,
    My favorite Christmas song is Rudolf.
    What's yours?
    I bet you like jingle bells. That one is a lot older.
                            Jordan
                            [age 6]

Dear God,

I like your signs.

                            Love,
                            Maria
                            [age 5]

Dear God,
    Here is five things I would like to see changed.
    Number 1—Mass
    Number 2—Bad nuns
    Number 3—War
    Number 4—Television
    Number 5—Make Christmas every week.
                            I could be your agent,
                            Donny
                            [age 12]

Dear God,

Did the Jews start Chanukah to go along with Christmas or did something really happen back there in the ancient days?

My friend told me about that lamp story. That was pretty good.

Best wishes,
Steve
[age 12]

Dear God,

Was Jesus born in a manger because there was no Holiday Inns in those years?

Only kidding,
Your pal Ricky
[age 10]

Dear God,

My bat mitzvah is only nine months away. Please think about me.

I hope we can meet. I'll be the red-haired girl who looks scared.

Shana
[age 12]

Dear Special Person,
    Thank you for Christmas, Easter, and for summer.
Also thanks for being with me.
    My next birthday is July 16. Mark it down.
                You are neat,
                Ryan
                [age 7]

DEAR God,
    Did you put All Saints Day near Holloween to give
all the sides an equal chance? Hah hah.
                I am going to be a monk
                on Holloween. Fooled
                you.
                Fitz
                [age 11]

Dear Hashem,
    As you probably know I am Jewish.
    I am small for my age. I way only 76 pounds.
    Is it okay if I don't fast all the way on Yom Kippur?
                This would help,
                Jay
                [age 10]
I would like to have only soda and potato chips for energy, maybe?

Dear God,
    What is franks and cents? Was it an old kind of money?

                        Maybe it was food?
                        Todd
                        [age 7]

Dear God,
    In the Holy Land, what do you do about snow for Christmas? That must be different and kind of weird.

                        Love ya God,
                        Bobby
                        [age 9]

Dear God,
    Is there a Christmas in Russia?
    They got nerve. They must have stole it from us.

                        Mad, real mad
                        Jimmy K.
                        [age 11]

Dear Sky God,
    Do you have holidays on the moon?
    I bet you eat lots of cheese there with dinner.

                        Captain Kirk
                        [age 12]

Santa Claus, the reindeer, and God,
I am going to catch you. I am going to make you stay for cereal and milk.
I like Lucky Charms. You can have Cherios. Rudolph can have red cereal.
See you,
Alex
[age 5]
My mom helped me spell this.

Dear God—Who I believe In.
Do you celebrate July 4 or do you just go wild on religion holidays?
If you do not you should.
We have a picnic here.

X X X

Carey
[age 10]

Dear God,
For Thanksgiving do you have a big deal in heaven? Or something else. Or do you just visit somebody's family in New England?
You can come here,
Elizabeth
Wellesley, ma
[age 9]

Dear God,
I know my mother and father give the things on Xmas, but I still think you must be the inspiration.
Thanks. Keep giving them ideas.

> Yours truly, at Xmas and
> always,
> Danielle
> [age 12]

Dear God,
Why don't you put Columbus in the Bible? (We get it off from school?)
Was it because he traveled a lot and this made it hard to get the story write?

> Samantha
> [age 9]

Dear God,
What is a Greek Orthodox?
I hear they have a different year than we have. How can that be?
Do you cover them too?

> Felicia
> [age 10]

Dear God,
Thank you for the ESPRIT sweater and shirt for Christmas. I knew they had ESPRIT in heaven!!!!
Love you!!!!
Julie
[age 11]

Dear God,
Is it a big letdown for you after Christmas? What about Santa?
What do you do on new years eve and the day too? Or is that old hats to you buy now after a million years?
Carlton
[age 10]

Dear God,
I think it is really cool the way you made such a big day for your son and had the whole world give gifts and all. But I think you should be fair and have days for the apostels too.
Petermas   Paulmas   Andymas
Even Judasmas would be good. Everyone should get a 2ND chance.
Merry Christmas,
Andy
[age 11]

Dear God,
SHALOM. Last Passover we ate Matzoh on everything. I mean Everything.
Couldn't we just eat toast? SHALOM.
Your good girl,
Sari
[age 9]

Dear God,
You are the best.
Easter is the best holiday.
Jesus's resurrection is the best story. I saw it in a movie once. It was the best vampire movie I ever saw.
Love,
Arn
[age 7]

Dear God,
I am Lutheran and two of my best friends are Jewish. One other is different all together. He is from India.
I think that it is not right that you left them out of Christmas. Please put them back in. They are very kind to me.

—Love always—
Ann
[age 9]

"Could You Please Change the Taste of Asparagus, God?"

Dear God,
   Do you have telephones in heaven? My number is
555-6392. What is yours? I get home from school about
three-thirty everyday.
                                   I'll talk to you,
                                   Martha
                                   [age 8]

Dear Creator,
   I think the best thing you ever invented was cartoons. All the kids I know love 'em.
                                   Hello from Detroit,
                                   Dan
                                   [age 7]

Dear God,
   My dad drinks beer. It looks kind of gross.
   Did King Solomon drink beer?
                                   Stanley,
                                   [age 10]

Dear God,
   DON'T GIVE UP ON US AND WE WON'T FOR-
GET ABOUT YOU.
                                   Anonymous,
                                   [age 11]

Dear God, Mary, and Family,
    Merry Christmas to all of you and all your relatives.
That means Jesus and Peter too.
                            Love,
                            Cynthia Sykes
                            12 Treadmill Road
                            [age 7]

Dear God,
    I think Mrs. Nancy Reagan is a real nice lady. She
likes kids. Is she anything like the Virgin Mary?
    God bless her.
                            Love,
                            Eve
                            [age 8]

To God/ Send it Federal Express
    Hope this gets to you by 1999. Otherwise I get my
stamp back. Guaranteed!
                            Your pen pal,
                            Dawn
                            [age 11]

Dear God,
I have doubts about you sometimes. Sometimes I really believe. Like when I was four and I hurt my arm and you healed it up fast. But my question is, if you could do this why don't you stop all the bad in the world? Like war. Like diseases. Like famine. Like drugs.
And there are problems in other people's neighborhoods too.

I'll try to believe more,
Ian
[age 10]

Dear God,
YOU ARE FANTASTIC!!!! Send me your autograph. Write it to
To my favorite person in America, who is the hansomest and smartest too, who all the girls want.

Over and out,
Bert
[age 9]

Sign it with a great big ᎒ and a lightning bolt. So all the kids will believe it's really you.

Dear God,

I wish I could spend all my time with you. We could go to beautiful places together. Like Paris. We could fill all the world with love. We could make every kid and grownup smile.

I don't think you can do it alone. Why don't you make me a special helper? My family and my teachers will understand. I am willing to give up some kids' stuff. It will be for a very good cause. How about it?

> With all the love in my
> heart,
> Marti
> [age 9]

P.S. I would like to take my
pink and white dress
with me, if that is okay.

Dear God,

When Christy Brinkley had a baby were you involved?

> Cordially,
> Ronald
> [age 9]

I just found out that Billy Joel was her husband.

Dear God,
    I voted for you in this year's all star game.
See:

                <u>Outfielders</u>
            ☒ Dave Winfield
            ☒ Jim Rice
            ☒ <u>_God_</u>

    I did not know which league to put you in, so I put
you in the American. We can't lose with you.
                    Hope it gives you a
                    laugh,
                    Tommy
                    [age 11]

Dear God,
    What do you think of kings and queens like Prince
Charles and Queen Di?
    I think they are snobs, if you ask me.
                    No hard feelings,
                    Ernie
                    [age 11]

Dear God,
    Can you get me into a soap opera?
                    Love and kisses,
                    Betty
                    [age 8]

Dear God in heaven,
Thank you so much for helping my two years old brother stop peaing in his pants. My whole family is relieved!

Thank you,
Lorissa
[age 6]

Dear "God,"
How did you get the name Earth? Ever think of changing it?
I'd like to see it called Tom's World.

Tom
[age 11]

Dear God,
Do you believe in spirits and ghosts? What about things in outer space? I don't but my friend Ed says their all around. I think Ed is weird.

Your friend too,
Robert
[age 11]

Dear God,
   Could you change the taste of asparagus?
   Everything thing else is OK.
                              Love,
                              Fred
                              [age 9]

Dear God,
   In the beginning of everything, you said let there be
light. Right? How did this feel? I would like to know.
   It must have been strange to have night all the time.
Like in Alaska. But I guess you must have been used to it.
What made you turn the switch?
   I live in Connecticut. Please keep the light here.
                              Thank you,
                              Arlene
                              [age 8]

Dear Big God,
   I think that you look like a big monster. But you do
good things for people. Like feasts and famine.
                              You make me laugh,
                              Diane
                              [age 10]

Dear God,
   My mother said we used to eat fish on Fridays. Did you stop it because of the smell?
                              Very truly yours,
                              Christa
                              [age 11]

Dear God and Jesus,
   I'm a big follower of you guys. I root for you both all the time. Keep those miracles coming.
                              Your best friend,
                              Stephen
                              [age 8]

Dear God,

Hello.

I hate people who say too much.
                              Emily
                              [age 10]

To Whom It May Concern,
   I want to believe in you real hard. But I don't know
how. My mom does but my dad does not. How can I
know for sure? Why don't you make things easier? It
would be nice. Nothing special. You don't have to part
the sea or nothing. Just something easy.
   Like have me turn thirteen sooner.
                              Joan
                              [age 12]

Dear God,
   I saw the Grand Canyon last summer. Nice piece of
work.
                              Love,
                              Alan
                              [age 9]

Dear GOD,
   I think that you very kind and generous.
   Can you see if I can get a bigger allowance?
                              Mike
                              [age 11]

Dear God,
    I don't really belive in you but I'm supposed to write a letter so here goes.
    Also I want to get in a book.
    If you are real why don't you prove it by appearing to me?
    I'll be on Schoolhouse Road at 5 O'CLOCK tomorrow.
    We'll see.

Laura
[age 9]

Dear Lord,
    You and I have something in common.
    We both have a lot of names.
    You have Lord
            God
            Jesus
            Father.

Signed,
Rodney William Peter
Johnson, Junior
[age 8]

Please look ⟶ I also have a nickname. It is Rodent.
What's yours?

Dear God,
    In school we read all there about Jesus being born.
One part I did not understand.
What is a mackulet decepsion?
                Love,
                Phyllis
                [age 10]

Dear Only God,
    You light up my life. So do mom and dad.

I hope you like this.   Luv,
I am not sure what it   Toni
means.   [age 7]

Dear God,
    Thank you for sending Doctor Heller to ask me
questions about you. He is very nice and we are becoming friends now.
    But he looks too young to be a doctor. He looks
more like an actor.
    Maybe he was in a Bible movie.
                Love,
                Connie
                [age 10]

Dear God,
    I read that home is where God (that's you) is.
    What does that mean, I wonder?
    Does it mean if I am at religious school I am not
away from home?
    Do I have to be in our living room to be with you?
    Are you everywhere?
    I am not sure. I just know that you are in my heart.
                                    From home,
                                    David
                                    [age 12]

Dear God,
    Did you know that our money says on it
                IN YOU WE TRUST?
    You must be rich.
                                    Take it easy,
                                    Your friend Jimmy
                                    [age 9]